Critical Data Storytelling for Libraries

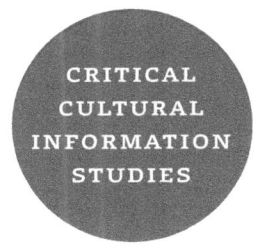

CRITICAL
CULTURAL
INFORMATION
STUDIES

CRITICAL DATA STORYTELLING FOR LIBRARIES

Crafting Ethical Narratives for Advocacy and Impact

Kate McDowell

ALA
Neal-Schuman

Chicago | 2025

Critical Cultural Information Studies is a book series to help advance the library field's discussions and understanding of often difficult issues, such as structural racism, equity, sexuality, disability, oppression, privilege, power, intersectionality, and inclusion and belonging.

Nicole A. Cooke is the series editor of Critical Cultural Information Studies. Cooke is the Augusta Baker Endowed Chair and associate professor at the School of Information Science at the University of South Carolina.

CCIS ADVISORY BOARD

ISBNs
979-8-89255-280-6 (paper)
979-8-89255-266-0 (PDF)

Library of Congress Cataloging-in-Publication Data
Names: McDowell, Kate author
Title: Critical data storytelling for libraries : crafting ethical narratives for advocacy and impact / Kate McDowell.
Description: Chicago : ALA Neal-Schuman, 2025. | Series: Critical cultural information studies | Includes bibliographical references and index.
Identifiers: LCCN 2025017296 | ISBN 9798892552806 paperback
Subjects: LCSH: Library statistics | Information visualization | Storytelling | Communication in library science | Libraries—Aims and objectives
Classification: LCC Z669.8 .M38 2025 | DDC 027.62/51—dc23/eng/20250604
LC record available at https://lccn.loc.gov/2025017296

Book design in the Leo, Brother 1816, and Laski Slab typefaces. Cover design by Alejandra Diaz.

♾ This paper meets the requirements of ANSI/NISO Z39.48-1992 (Permanence of Paper).

Printed in the United States of America

29 28 27 26 25   5 4 3 2 1

This book is dedicated to the FEARLESS WARRIORS
who understand the power of words and learning
and the freedom from tyranny that libraries must represent.

Contents

Prologue

As I was finishing this book, I received one of many notifications that my grant was terminated. This followed the March 14, 2025, executive order by President Trump empowering the Department of Government Efficiency (DOGE) to destroy the Institute of Museum and Library Services (IMLS). All the hardworking staff were put on leave and given "Reduction in Force" notices that described their jobs as "abolished." Losing an institution like the IMLS is only one of many frightening and devastating losses of stability and security for people in the United States.

The struggles of this past month have many times brought to mind my grandfather Frank B. Parsons (aka Papa Frank). He came home from World War II having seen a kind of injustice that changed his already generous spirit and opened his eyes. As the city attorney of Fairfield, Alabama, in the 1960s, when the Ku Klux Klan spread flyers declaring that they were planning a march, Mr. Parsons defended the city and won, all the way up to the Alabama Supreme Court in 1962. Then he argued the case before the US Supreme Court in 1963, and he lost. He never stopped working for justice. My mother and uncles described his law office waiting room as one of the most integrated places in the Birmingham region. In a context where racism was rampant and normative, he practiced law to help others, no matter their race or income. I remember people stopping by the house in the summer with vegetables as thanks, and one of my uncles remembers a man bringing "payment" in socks. Papa Frank also served on the school board and advocated for desegregation while my grandmother Mama Lib served on the library board and advocated for literacy for all. At his funeral, the First United Methodist Church in Fairfield was overflowing with the most integrated crowd I ever saw during all our visits to Alabama.

We win some, we lose some, but we keep going.

People have always been called to do extremely hard things in the face of hatred and injustice. For example, the women who established library services in the late nineteenth century conducted national surveys to make their case at a time when their gender kept them from speaking aloud at American Library Association (ALA) meetings. In the face of this current wave of fear and the specific targeting of libraries, library work becomes more important than ever. Where can citizens turn when they find themselves bewildered by online forms? Who will help when benefits are suddenly suspended or ended without warning? Where else can people turn when they need to be cool in the heat or warm in the cold? Libraries are one of the only places left in the United States where entry requires neither buying something nor believing something. Keeping them open will require data storytelling of the highest caliber, and this volume is a start toward strengthening our specific stories. Because, win or lose, libraries as institutions must survive.

—Kate McDowell, April 2025

Acknowledgments

This book would not have been possible without the support, encouragement, and guidance of more people than I can possibly name here. First and foremost, I want to express my deep appreciation to Nicole Cooke for suggesting this project and planting the seed that grew into this book. My deepest thanks to my editor, Rachel Chance, for believing in this work from the start, and to Samantha Kundert for her phenomenal editing skills that brought this book through writing and into life. The Core Design Team and focus group participants for the Data Storytelling Toolkit for Libraries (DSTL) project helped shape my thinking and kept me focused on practical applications. Deep appreciation to the Institute of Museum and Library Services for funding the DSTL as an out-of-the-box creative project, not just once but twice, albeit with unexpected termination the second time. Katie Kritikos served as initial development editor, capably connecting my broad ideas to the specific library audience, and I am so grateful.

Several institutions hosted me during the sabbatical writing process. To Maggie Taylor and the team at Delight Flower Farm for the 2023–2024 residency, your space provided the inspiration and blossoms I needed to get through the first draft of chapter 5. At Aarhus University's Center for Critical Data Practices, I owe a great deal to Director Magda Tyzlik-Carver and the inspiration of her "data fermentation" workshop. Much appreciation goes to the welcoming team at DARC and the School of Communication and Culture, especially Søren Pold, for his generous hosting, providing me with a real intellectual home in Denmark—Tak for sidst, vi ses snart igen! Special thanks to Pablo Velasco and Karoline Vildlyng for their companionship and ideas about teaching and libraries, respectively. At the University of Bergen, the Center for Digital Narrative was an inspiring environment where I could instantly start talking about stories and storytelling all the time, and I am deeply appreciative of Scott Rettberg-Walker and Jill Rettberg-Walker for their sponsorship during my time in Norway. I must acknowledge the School of Information Sciences at the University of Illinois at Urbana-Champaign, my work-home for almost twenty years now, for approving the year-long sabbatical that made this book possible.

To my brilliant and insightful colleagues: Matthew Turk, Jill Naiman, Sara Goek, Madelyn Sanfilippo, Melissa Ocepek, Jodi Schneider, Mike Twidale, Karen Wickett, Liz Hoiem, Sara Schwebel, Kyungwon Koh, Rachel Magee, Sarah Park Dahlen, Sharon Comstock, Martin Wolske, and Jennifer Burek-Pierce—your academic companionship has been invaluable in weathering good times and bad. I would also like to thank the professors who supported me in joining their ranks: Stephen Miles (and Kathy Killion, also a stellar educator), Betsy Hearne, Christine Jenkins, Boyd Rayward, Don Latham, Brian Sturm, and Gary Burnett. Your insights and encouragement, past and present, continue to shape my academic and professional path.

To the friends who have seen me through so many ups and downs—Laurel, Elizabeth, Amy, Deborah, Rebecca, Julie, Celeste, Bea and the coffee group, and too many others to name—thank you. Thank you to all the Art Night companions—Jane, Beth, Emily, Kim, Azmi, Ezra, and more—for our every Wednesday playfulness and deliciousness. I am constantly remade by the love of our Urbana community. To my dear friend and bestie Danielle, whose dedication to changing the world every day is an inspiration—your tireless fight for justice, insights, and wisdom means the world to me.

I am very grateful to my family: my mother Betty, my father Hugh, and my brother Daniel (Danny) McDowell who have heard me and seen me through so many phases of life and career before I came to land on the path where I am now, where I belong. I am so grateful for the ways you celebrate my work—it helps me to keep on keeping on! To my amazing aunts and uncles, I am so lucky to have you on my team.

Finally, to the love of my life, Ben Grosser, you are the sweetest human I have ever known and the most incredible international artist I will ever meet. Your generosity, creativity, genius, and constant love have made all of this possible. The way you bring your sensitivity to keep fighting against the emotional desolation of big tech fuels me to keep fighting for libraries and reading. Thank you for being my constant source of strength and inspiration, and for being my companion on all the journeys, now and forever.

Introduction
Storytelling and Better Information Futures

The Need for Storytelling in Librarianship

At a recent storytelling workshop, someone approached me to ask for help. She told me that she didn't really have any stories. It was in the fall, so I asked, "What happened this summer?" She said there was a big renovation project at her library: a massive overhaul of how the collection was organized, the staffing that handled shelving, and even the shelves themselves. I asked a bit more about why and how it had happened, and it turned out there had been a successful fundraising campaign, showing overwhelming support for the public library in these times since the pandemic. A wave of new donations had paid for new infrastructure, and equally importantly, had supported administrative time and focus to really design and implement major changes. I said, "You mean that donations let you change how your library works for the community?" "Yes," she said. "But is that really a story?"

Yes, that is really a story. In fact, it's an amazing story, and it's also the kind of story that happens every day, all the time when citizens get together to support their local public library.

Storytelling has a history in librarianship that stretches back over 130 years as a live, oral, interpretive art that has been a crucial practice in library services to young people (Alvey 1974). This tradition emphasizes the relationship between teller and audience and respect for the story and its source (Hearne 1993). Such a relationship occurs in the moment of storytelling, establishing trust and goodwill between librarians and those who come to the library to hear stories told and find favorite narratives (Del Negro 2017). There is tremendous potential for librarians to mobilize what they know from captivating audiences of children, parents, and caregivers week after week, year after year, to support the libraries themselves.

The gap in creating meaningful and effective data storytelling for libraries is twofold.

First, most people treat work stories as ephemeral, passed around inside the organization informally, without ways of capturing those stories for outside audiences as well. The stories we tell about the power of libraries, for example, should be told and retold over time, with the input of attentive audiences, so that they become memorable and highly retellable. Stories about any information organization can start organically, as informal moments of sharing—consider coworkers talking about a surprisingly high attendance at an event or an unusual percentage increase in service usage. Informal conversations about what professionals learn tend to be ephemeral, with only reports capturing this data for larger audiences. However, these stories can have greater impact when they are captured and crafted with the kind of compelling supporting evidence that only data storytelling can provide. This will involve a careful consideration of issues such as whether to use raw attendance/usage number increases or the percentage of people impacted in a community. With so many competing pressures for time and attention, many professionals tend to frame data-gathering for reports as one-time events, with one set of "snapshot" findings to describe. The idea of a longer-term organizational story challenges us to interweave data collection and reporting with broader data storytelling. Structuring information in story form makes data easier to remember, along with its context and meaning. The best stories are told many times to audience after audience, honing their form into something that is easy to remember and share. The data we collect about our libraries deserves attentive reflection, which is part of *critical data storytelling*. Considering our data through a storytelling lens has great potential to take ephemeral stories and make them memorable and meaningful to larger audiences.

Second, it is difficult to think in terms of stories. We are all storytellers, but it is not always easy to translate data into a story. Librarians bring a deep love of story and outstanding abilities to make others' stories come alive, as in storytimes. However, it can be difficult to translate that joy and skill into meaningful ways of conceptualizing data storytelling. Even though librarians are typically incredible readers who consume and talk about stories constantly, it requires a new conceptual frame to look at the stories they know and enjoy for their potential as a resource for narrative strategies. This book builds on the skills of effective librarianship so that librarians can take ephemeral data presentations or reports and make them memorable and meaningful to larger audiences. When organizations collect, analyze, and store data, do they create compelling stories about what is learned over time? The evidence we have—what we do, who we are, whose lives libraries change—is the basis of our most important stories. Surveys that are repeated lend themselves to stories of institutional continuity or transformation, and librarians can leverage diligent data collection alongside the 130-year history of library storytelling to communicate information and emotion, to interweave the two and extend our passion for family literacy to a passion for public data literacy. If the data, the information synthesized from data, and the prior stories told about that data are accessible, then, as time moves on, new storytellers in new roles can tell stories about institutional continuity or transformation. Data storytelling might become the most important part of an organization's historical record for advocacy.

These two issues—story ephemerality and the challenge of thinking in story— are sometimes delegated to communications professionals. A library might have a marketing department (or one person) that knows and does marketing effectively. However, marketing professionals are customer- and community-facing, but not always stakeholder-facing. For example, marketers are not in the business of convincing library boards to vote in support of a proposed change to policy, budget, or services. Librarian expertise is needed to support this kind of change-making, through persuasion and lobbying—they might argue, for example, to modify policies to provide more flexibility in collections and materials loan periods or renewals in the face of long-lasting changes after a pandemic. Even when marketing can help, the availability of dedicated staff in libraries is extremely uneven and is rarely aligned with the growing economic inequities that impact communities across the United States. While marketing can be valuable, and there will be some marketing professionals who are exceptional individuals, marketing is not designed to go deep enough to communicate the library's mission to those who have the power to fund or defund organizations. Library leaders must be effective data storytellers.

Data storytelling for community advocacy and social justice has an important history and much future potential in librarianship, but there can be real challenges with this work. There are nuances of communicating powerfully about social injustices while also respectfully representing communities that would benefit the most from greater social justice. To do data storytelling well means to engage with issues of equity and avoid the common pitfall of overgeneralizing about people based on data so that we reproduce stereotypes. Along with data storytelling, we must also engage critical approaches and introduce critical storytelling. Data can dehumanize people, especially when full and rich lives are represented only as numbers (Slovic 2007). This book is about exploring the storytelling heart and transforming it for everyday library advocacy, offering guidance to librarians who want to tell impactful library data stories but don't know where to start.

Effective and Ethical Data Storytelling

This book sparks a larger critical conversation about storytelling and the real-world skills and abilities that are needed for library data storytelling to be effective and ethical. Over the past six years, I have led a growing team of instructors at the University of Illinois in developing courses in data storytelling for library and information science (LIS) and other graduate students and for information science undergraduates. Through this process, we have developed a set of robust conceptual approaches that are adaptable to any kind of critical data storytelling. In this book, I adapt my data storytelling instruction for the audience of information professionals, based on my storytelling consulting and input from colleagues in libraries across the nation. This book is also the result of years of teaching and consulting about storytelling with nonprofit organizations. My insights are also based on more than 100 interviews with information professionals about their storytelling practices; studies of student projects in storytelling and data storytelling courses; and talks and workshops with librarians and other information professionals in higher education, information technology, advancement and fundraising, and more.

Other books provide library data visualization with specific examples for guidance (Magnuson 2016) or real-world examples of and conceptual models for data-driven communication (Riche et al. 2018). Still other programmatic "storytelling with data" books and courses provide prescriptive fundamentals for data in visual communication (Knaflic 2015). This prior research, however, lacks a critical approach; it does not engage story in depth, and it ignores the history, use, and power of storytelling to represent (or misrepresent) communities. This book centers critical storytelling and commits to understanding power dynamics from a storytelling perspective. It is not just a how-to guide to storytelling using data; it is a why-to guide to storytelling that incorporates a critical perspective on how storytelling can enact and perpetuate both inclusions and exclusions. But before we explore critical data storytelling further, we must first unpack some essential terms, concepts, and theories.

Defining Critical Data Storytelling ——————————————

Critical data storytelling is a new approach that entails a commitment to understanding power dynamics from a storytelling perspective, but to define critical data storytelling, we must first define several terms related to data storytelling.

Data Storytelling

Data storytelling means any communication of data that draws upon narrative structures or strategies so that an audience can remember the information in story form. Data storytelling is a practice of making data and the information gleaned from it accessible, meaningful, and clear to audiences. From taxpaying citizens to boards of trustees and the governmental agencies that distribute funding, from library users to national or international granting agencies, data is valuable for understanding the landscape of libraries and related information data is valuable for understanding how a particular library connects or compares with similar institutions. Data is valuable for making compelling arguments about who is and is not being served and how services need to improve so that libraries can reach everyone. To fully understand these definitions of data storytelling, it is important to step back and define story.

Story

A *story* is both narratively patterned information and a narrative experience. Narratively patterned information is easiest to understand as a classic way of telling stories: patterns like stories of transformation or stories of carrying on through hardship. In a story, "language must be structured by the chronology of narrative (beginning, middle, and end) and the logic of narrative (character, setting, and plot). This definition invokes two intellectual traditions: (1) the beginning-middle-end structure of folktales and their centrality in LIS discourses about story aesthetics and categorization, and (2) the logic of narrative as defined in semiotics" (McDowell 2021, 3). Semiotics is the structural study of meaning, breaking down meaning into its smallest components—semes—to understand how meaning is constructed. In addition to these structural ways of understanding story, story is also an experience of narrative. Narrative experience is lived and embodied, such as when the "reception of collective interpretation can be viscerally sensed through live audience responses—laughter, applause, boos, hisses, gasps, sighs" (McDowell 2021, 3). Stories are constituted through narrative experience, and audiences are partly constitutive of the stories told to or with them. In other words, good storytellers respond in real time to their audiences, adjusting their delivery of meaning while remaining true to their data.

Critical Approaches and Critical Theory

Critical data storytelling brings the concepts of narratively patterned information and narrative experience together with one more set of ideas: that people are impacted by the social conditions of their lives in ways that determine whether they have the power to change them. This approach is *critical*, which means to think rationally and with healthy skepticism about what is, what might be, and what should be. *Critical approaches* ask questions about how things work, and why, in order to understand, analyze what is, and propose ways to make things better. *Critical theory* focuses on understanding power, who has it, how it operates, and its consequences for people's lives.

Critical theory has a long history. It stretches from long before the Frankfurt School philosophers (Arato and Gebhardt 1982), whose prescient concerns about mass media in the 1930s seem eerily applicable in the era of internet misinformation. It has continued to Kimberlé Crenshaw's critical race theory scholarship (1989) that questions the uneven, legal distribution of power based on race and racism in the United States, and beyond. More recently, the term *critical theory* has become politically polarized (and chapter 4 covers polarized audiences in greater depth). In general, any time leaders try to keep citizens from questioning how power works, citizens can develop a critical approach to assert their right to ask questions. More specifically, information professionals should be critical and vocal any time legislatures outlaw words, books, or ways of thinking. Because storytelling is powerful, and because stories justify power imbalance, critical theory is key to understanding the applications of data storytelling for library advocacy.

Critical Thinking in Information Organizations

For anyone working in an information organization, critical thinking is already a crucial part of designing information access, systems, and services. Critical thinking is how we make things better and fulfill our mission and core values.

Every time we engage topics of information, literacy, and intellectual freedom, we think critically about who has access to information, who does not, what barriers are standing in the way, and how those barriers could be removed. For example, reading the American Library Association's (ALA's) Library Bill of Rights (ala.org/advocacy/intfreedom/librarybill) provides an exercise in critical thinking about what it means to be a person in a free society. The Library Bill of Rights enshrines some of librarianship's professional ideals, such as challenging censorship, and how or whether these ideals apply in a particular setting requires thinking critically about how libraries are (or are not) living up to them. And whether we think of these concepts as theory or just plain common sense, the ability to be critical is directly linked with making progress or improvements.

Critical Data Storytelling Framework

Critical data storytelling is the framework for this book, combining evidence with narrative strategies in critical ways to advocate for the best possible information services for citizens and communities. The best possible information services are not abstract, but instead are the concrete products of a continual negotiation between the ideals of the librarianship profession and the realities of specific contexts and situations, from buildings to budgets. Quantitative and qualitative data collection provides the evidence that we can interpret in story form using narrative strategies that later chapters outline in detail, while critical approaches to advocacy ensure that the understanding of communities is accurate and rich.

Applying Critical Librarianship to Critical Data Storytelling

Critical data storytelling draws from other perspectives, including *critical librarianship*, which calls for thinking about power in libraries and the design of all their systems and services (Accardi et al. 2010; Nicholson and Seale 2018). According to Robinson (2019), "In information science, critical librarianship seeks to disrupt normative approaches to library work by confronting these ideologies and systems, empowering both library workers and users to understand how these structures affect the access and dissemination of information." Critical thinking for data storytelling also means questioning how data is generated, how it is interpreted, who is represented (and left out), how social biases impact representations that translate into unequal services, and how we can create more justice in information practices and institutions. This approach draws from data feminism, which emphasizes that data is not neutral or objective, it is too often computationally de-contextualized, and it never speaks for itself (D'Ignazio and Klein 2020). Finally, critical data storytelling should include a thoughtful approach to respectful representation of the story itself, including how it is shared, when, and with whom. Stories are not neutral but come with histories, contexts, and cultural origins so that not all stories are every person's to tell. The teller's perspective and standpoint must also be scrutinized in data storytelling.

Applying Critical Race and Feminist Theories to Critical Data Storytelling

From other critical perspectives like critical race and feminist theories, storytelling is a bridge for marginalized voices to be heard in normatively exclusive spaces. Communicating the effects of marginalization from a marginalized perspective requires much strength from willing storytellers and a commitment to listening from audiences. For example, from the marginalized perspective of a woman of color, speaking about the impact of marginalization requires strategic approaches to avoid being dismissed as, for example, angry. These things are easy to say but difficult to do, and the intellectual and emotional labor that goes into any work of telling silenced stories should never be underestimated (Moraga et al. 1983). A serious consideration of storytelling as information practice—and as a vehicle for our most organizationally significant information—is yet another among a host of practices that are necessary to make room for a greater representation of previously silenced voices in the information professions. Centering story and storytelling as fundamental to library advocacy calls for a richer variety of stories, data, tellers, and audiences for a future of greater inclusion. Conceptually, storytelling bridges ways of knowing that are usually separate. In the information sciences, epistemologies are ways of knowing that frame what we believe to be true. Storytelling bridges a socially constructed way of knowing with an evidence-focused way of knowing (McDowell 2021). These are often divided; think of the humanistic social interplay of learning new ideas in children's storytimes and how different this is from the implicit positivist orientation of computational systems that gather data stripped of any social context. When we move beyond the dismissal of stories as only emotional, then we can consider stories for both their informational and emotional content, taking seriously what people know and learn from stories and through storytelling.

Research on Storytelling in Librarianship

Despite more than a century of practice, library storytelling has been largely overlooked for its research and epistemological implications and been "neglected as a source for new ways of thinking and knowing" (McDowell 2020, 94). There are a few studies that engage storytelling in LIS, with youth or otherwise, demonstrating the educational and social-emotional benefits of oral storytelling (Agosto 2013). In exploring why storytelling matters, an analysis of children's responses to oral storytelling revealed benefits in visualization, cognitive engagement, critical thinking, and story-sequencing abilities (Agosto 2016). Textbooks on storytelling have sometimes glossed over the power imbalances between the cultures from which stories come and those who take them for retelling (MacDonald 1993). Storytelling for young people, especially the retelling of stories from folklore crossing cultural boundaries, requires careful consideration to distinguish between sharing, borrowing, and stealing (Hearne 1999, Hearne 2011).

Storytelling is compelling, and narrative can powerfully affect our brains; from LIS research, we know that stories can entrance listeners, with shared states of trance-like attention among audience members (Sturm 1999). Beyond librarianship, neurological research finds that neural story processing involves a "mirroring process of embodied subjectivity" or experiences of "narrative emotions" that are predicated on story's "ability to intertwine our experience of time" (Armstrong 2020, 93). Specialized mirror neurons in the brain contribute to experiencing empathy through story (Rizzolatti 2008), and contextual empathy cues increase the potential for empathetic experience through story (Roshanaei et al. 2019).

A few qualitative studies have explored librarians' perceptions and uses of storytelling. Youth services librarians value storytelling for its use in motivating reading, encouraging imagination through vicarious experience, sharing culture and history, building personal relationships, sparking emotional engagement, and more (Sturm and Nelson 2016). Organizational storytelling among academic reference librarians conveys rich tacit knowledge and can help explain work conditions, provide warning systems, afford shared preparation for work challenges, and more (Colón-Aguirre 2015). Qualitative studies like these draw on Elfreda Chatman's work exploring the lived experiences of information, revealing boundaries between "life-worlds" that are essential to understanding how people are informed and, ultimately, what they know as individuals within groups (Chatman 1996). While Chatman's work does not always use the term *critical*, it is informed by the same fundamental questions about whose voices are heard and not heard, as are those who have critiqued (Garner 2022) and extended (Jaeger and Burnett 2010; Gray 2022) her work.

Epistemologies for Better Information Futures

Definitions of *data* and *information* typically rely on an empiricist epistemology that excludes social complexities like "opinions, intentions, desires" and "cultural forms and social practices" (Ma 2012, 722). Data is treated as neutral, objective, and devoid of context, when in fact "it is the context that makes the data possible" (D'Ignazio and Klein 2020, 152). Data is only the input that is interpreted as information, and data is entirely limited by the context of its collection. Furthermore, various cultural and social exclusions in LIS abound, ranging from microaggressions to epistemicide, so that some social complexities are more likely to be studied while others are ignored. Storytelling can bridge these epistemological divides, but only if there is room for contradicting the stock stories that support the status quo (Bell 2010).

Confronting Epistemicide, Racism, and Colonialism in Storytelling

When stories are ignored, silenced, stolen, or their cultural context is betrayed, they may vanish along with the information and knowledge they contain. Epistemicide, or "the killing, silencing, annihilation, or devaluing of a knowledge system," and the harms of being told that some stories "do not count" have intergenerational impacts that information professionals must engage when "handling knowledge from every field" (Patin et al. 2021, 1306). When many stories are overwritten by only the few stories that "count," and when information professionals are accustomed to these epistemicides as everyday injustices, it may help to turn conceptually to storytelling as a way to understand the epistemological divides by which some human activities are considered viable information while others are dismissed as mere tales, myths, or superstitions.

Even worse, demands for storytelling can deepen the damage done by racism. Telling a story is not a simple matter when power differentials, such as historic and contemporary colonization, inform every aspect of whether the audience contains insiders or outsiders and how the story will be received. As Dian Million writes:

> The mainstream white society read Native stories through thick pathology narratives. Yet the same stories collectively witnessed the social violence that was and is colonialism's heart. Individually or collectively, these stories were hard to "tell." They were neither emotionally easy nor communally acceptable. Women (and men) who organized against family violence and politically sanctioned sex discrimination in their communities balanced the necessity to change things and constraints to "silence" their pain and experience. To "tell" called for a reevaluation of reservation and reserve beliefs about what was appropriate to say about your own family, your community. (Million 2009, 56)

When it comes to storytelling, as Eve Tuck and K. Wayne Yang (2012) wrote so poignantly, decolonization is not a metaphor.

Cultural Competence in Critical Storytelling

Critical storytelling approaches are not new, but narratology and critical theory tend to focus more on theorizing power imbalances rather than on critical practice. While what Michel Foucault (1966) calls "the order of things" and the "hidden network that determines the way they confront one another" (xxi) are important to consider, the task of any culturally competent librarian or information professional is not only to see power, but also to *reorder* things so that systems improve. Critical storytelling approaches are vital because library stories routinely "trip" over "color lines" (Honma 2005) by imagining that the equity that libraries idealize is the same as the equity they enact or represent. Advocacy storytelling therefore "trips" and backfires when it is not fully engaged with cultural competence and social justice, which chapter 1 discusses more fully. It is imperative to teach social justice storytelling so that students can confront injustices and "call in" the audience to do better with accurate and persuasive stories (McDowell and Cooke 2022).

Library advocacy storytelling is a crucial skill of librarianship in the twenty-first century, but not all stories belong to all peoples to tell. Storytelling is always embedded in layers of cultural contexts that include the potential for positive story-sharing as well as damaging story-stealing. Libraries as institutions regularly engage in advocacy storytelling, but those stories have impacts that may be more inclusive or more exploitative of the individuals and communities, depending on how data is framed and interpreted. Exposing and shaming nonconsensual stories abounds on the internet, yet we take too little account of these dynamics when it comes to issues like data-sharing and data literacy. Cultural competence and social justice in library storytelling must include knowing when to tell or refrain from telling others' stories as part of a serious consideration of storytelling dynamics and ethics.

Where We Begin: A Road Map to Critical Data Storytelling in Libraries

This text is a guidebook to critical data storytelling for information professionals from any background, especially librarians. This book is also for library data analysts, librarians, advocates for libraries, or anyone tasked with gathering, making sense of, and making arguments about what to do based on data. Leaders who want to make information organizations more just and inclusive will learn about the power of data storytelling for advocacy. Any information professionals who have data they need to communicate to audiences will benefit from a deeper understanding of critical data storytelling, as will those who work directly with data, storytelling, library advocacy, and social justice initiatives. Readers who recognize the power of data but struggle with narrative will learn narrative strategies, improving their competence in critically assessing power in storytelling exchanges. Those comfortable and familiar with storytelling will learn more about how to connect their stories with data for effective advocacy. For readers comfortable with both data and story, this book shares the critical dynamics of storytelling as both a skill and a key vehicle for inclusive and just information communication. Each chapter of this book focuses on theory and practice for using data storytelling critically and thoughtfully. Storytelling is a dynamic process, and chapter 1 starts by describing and defining *storytelling* as a triangle with six parts. First, there is the storyteller, the audience, and the story as it is told in that relationship. Then there are each of the relationships between these three: storyteller and audience, audience and story, and story and storyteller. The first chapter provides a conceptual grounding, defining storytelling practices that relate directly to professional applications in libraries and to a wide variety of other information professions as well.

Chapter 2 defines *library data* in relation to common and effective advocacy arguments and argues that we must put story before storage. Boards of trustees and citizens may tell different stories about the library, but they should all tell stories about the library that are grounded in library data. Implicit advocacy goals and motivations, however, often underlie the ways that we collect and analyze library data. They constitute the basis of our "classic" data stories. Understanding these goals and motivations and data that provide supporting evidence helps us not only make compelling stories from data, but also reframes the data we have already collected. By thinking about the dynamic storytelling triangle and its relationships—among teller, audience, and story—at the outset, we can align library data collection processes with long-term storytelling potential, prioritizing interaction over transaction. This alignment means that library data has a full life cycle—not just in collection and storage or visualization for a specific report, but for communication to all stakeholders.

Chapter 3 presents three time-honored and effective *narrative strategies* for organizing the informational and emotional content of library data stories. These three strategies—classic structures, plot, and iterative revision—are easy to adapt to any situation appropriate for the data being presented. Narratives can be built by (1) working intuitively and borrowing classic narrative structures, (2) focusing on data and plot development, and (3) following a process of iterative revision from data to wisdom. These ways can be combined; for example, a revision process can be used to improve a narrative built from classic structures or through plot development. While these strategies organize the flow of a story, they are perhaps most important for focusing on the story's meaning. Combining informational and emotional elements is the heart of effective story structure and considers the audience's experience of the story. This ensures that audiences can retell the stories that they hear and become library advocacy storytellers themselves.

Audiences matter, and chapter 4 explores *audience attitudes*, digging into the ways that contemporary patterns in communities present challenges for library data communication. Five kinds of attitudes each correspond to different approaches to tone and tactics. Maintaining a calm tone in the face of negativity or even the active spreading of disinformation about the library can be challenging. This is where the storyteller's own emotional experience is critically important to see, understand, and approach audiences both rationally and strategically. The anxiety that comes with storytelling to difficult audiences is profound. There is a reason why many people are afraid of public speaking. Thinking through how you will present yourself in terms of tone and what you will present in terms of tactics are ways of ensuring that the process of communicating to difficult audiences does not derail the story.

The past few years have revealed how difficult it can be to maintain open and transparent public communication in the face of rampant misinformation and active disinformation agents, whether humans or bots. Chapter 5 takes up the challenge of storytelling in an age of frequent, virulent *misinformation*. Drawing on analogies from COVID-19 misinformation research, this chapter considers book banning and the role of librarians and library advocates as storytellers against misinformation, by synthesizing some of the tactics that can be most effective in these difficult situations.

Critical data storytelling is a way of thinking that holds data-gathering processes to the highest ethical standards. It starts with understanding storytelling as both a tool and a process of creating a shared reality, based on at least enough trust to be willing to listen. This process begins with understanding the relationships between the teller, audience, and story.

REFERENCES

Accardi, Maria T., Emily Drabinski, and Alana Kumbier. 2010. *Critical Library Instruction: Theories and Methods.* Library Juice.

Agosto, Denise E. 2013. "If I Had Three Wishes: The Educational and Social/Emotional Benefits of Oral Storytelling." *Storytelling, Self, Society* 9, no. 1: 53–76. https://doi.org/10.13110/storselfsoci.9.1.0053.

Agosto, Denise E. 2016. "Why Storytelling Matters: Unveiling the Literacy Benefits of Storytelling." *Children and Libraries* 14, no. 2: 21–26. https://doi.org/10.5860/cal.14n2.21.

Alvey, Richard Gerald. 1974. "The Historical Development of Organized Storytelling to Children in the United States." Dissertation, University of Pennsylvania. https://repository.upenn.edu/dissertations/AAI7502695.

Arato, Andrew, and Eike Gebhardt. 1982. *The Essential Frankfurt School Reader.* Continuum.

Armstrong, Paul B. 2020. *Stories and the Brain: The Neuroscience of Narrative.* Johns Hopkins University Press.

Bell, Lee Anne. 2010. *Storytelling for Social Justice: Connecting Narrative and the Arts in Antiracist Teaching.* 2nd edition. Routledge. https://doi.org/10.4324/9780203852231.

Chatman, Elfreda A. 1996. "The Impoverished Life-World of Outsiders." *Journal of the American Society for Information Science* 47, no. 3: 193–206. https://doi.org/10.1002/(SICI)1097-4571(199603)47:3<193::AID-ASI3>3.0.CO;2-T.

Colón-Aguirre, Mónica. 2015. "Organizational Storytelling among Academic Reference Librarians." *Portal: Libraries and the Academy* 15, no. 2 (April): 233–50.

Crenshaw, Kimberlé. 1989. "Demarginalizing the Intersection of Race and Sex: A Black Feminist Critique of Antidiscrimination Doctrine, Feminist Theory and Antiracist Politics." *University of Chicago Legal Forum*, no. 1. https://chicagounbound.uchicago.edu/uclf/vol1989/iss1/8.

Del Negro, Janice. 2017. *Engaging Teens with Story: How to Inspire and Educate Youth with Storytelling*. Libraries Unlimited.

D'Ignazio, Catherine, and Lauren F. Klein. 2020. *Data Feminism*. MIT Press.

Foucault, Michel. 1966. *The Order of Things: An Archaeology of the Human Sciences*. Vintage Books.

Garner, Jane. 2022. "Taking Chatman Back to Prison: Rethinking the Theory of Life in the Round." *Journal of Documentation*. December. https://doi.org/10.1108/JD-09-2022-0192.

Gray, LaVerne. 2022. "Information Abundance and Deficit: Revisiting Elfreda Chatman's Inquiry of Marginal Spaces and Populations." *Journal of Critical Library and Information Studies* 3 (September). http://journals.litwinbooks.com/index.php/jclis/article/view/151.

Hearne, Betsy. 1993. "Respect the Source: Reducing Cultural Chaos in Picture Books, Part Two." *School Library Journal* 39, no. 8 (August) 33–37.

Hearne, Betsy. 1999. "Swapping Tales and Stealing Stories: The Ethics and Aesthetics of Folklore in Children's Literature." *Library Trends* 47, no. 3: 509–28.

Hearne, Betsy. 2011. "Folklore in Children's Literature: Contents and Discontents." In *Handbook of Research on Children's and Young Adult Literature*, edited by Shelby Wolf, Karen Coats, Patricia Enciso, and Christine Jenkins, 209–23. Routledge.

Honma, Todd. 2005. "Trippin' Over the Color Line: The Invisibility of Race in Library and Information Studies." *InterActions: UCLA Journal of Education and Information Studies* 1, no. 2. https://doi.org/10.5070/D412000540.

Jaeger, Paul T., and Gary Burnett. 2010. *Information Worlds: Social Context, Technology, and Information Behavior in the Age of the Internet*. New York: Routledge. https://doi.org/10.4324/9780203851630.

Knaflic, Cole Nussbaumer. 2015. *Storytelling with Data: A Data Visualization Guide for Business Professionals*. Wiley.

Ma, Lai. 2012. "Meanings of Information: The Assumptions and Research Consequences of Three Foundational LIS Theories." *Journal of the*

American Society for Information Science and Technology 63, no. 4 (April): 716–23.

MacDonald, Margaret Read. 1993. *The Storyteller's Start-up Book: Finding, Learning, Performing, and Using Folktales, Including Twelve Tellable Tales*. August House.

Magnuson, Lauren, ed. 2016. *Data Visualization: A Guide to Visual Storytelling for Libraries*. Rowman & Littlefield.

McDowell, Kate. 2020. "Storytelling, Young Adults, and Three Paradoxes." In *Transforming Young Adult Services, Second Edition*, edited by Anthony Bernier, 93–109. American Library Association.

McDowell, Kate. 2021. "Storytelling Wisdom: Story, Information, and DIKW." *Journal of the Association for Information Science and Technology* 72, no. 10, Special issue: "Paradigm Shift in the Field of Information" (March): 1223–33. https://doi.org/10.1002/asi.24466.

McDowell, Kate, and Nicole A. Cooke. 2022. "Social Justice Storytelling: A Pedagogical Imperative." *The Library Quarterly* 92, no. 4 (October): 355–78. https://doi.org/10.1086/721391.

Million, Dian. 2009. "Felt Theory: An Indigenous Feminist Approach to Affect and History." *Wicazo Sa Review* 24, no. 2: 53–76. www.jstor.org/stable/40587781.

Moraga, Cherríe, Gloria Anzaldúa, and Toni Cade Bambara. 1983. *This Bridge Called My Back: Writings by Radical Women of Color*. 2nd edition. Kitchen Table, Women of Color.

Nicholson, Karen P., and Maura Seale. 2018. *The Politics of Theory and the Practice of Critical Librarianship*. Litwin Books.

Patin, Beth, Melinda Sebastian, Jieun Yeon, Danielle Bertolini, and Alexandra Grimm. 2021. "Interrupting Epistemicide: A Practical Framework for Naming, Identifying, and Ending Epistemic Injustice in the Information Professions." *Journal of the Association for Information Science and Technology* 72, no. 10: 1306–18. https://doi.org/10.1002/asi.24479.

Riche, Nathalie Henry, Christophe Hurter, Nicholas Diakopoulos, and Sheelagh Carpendale, eds. 2018. *Data-Driven Storytelling*. A K Peters/CRC. https://doi.org/10.1201/9781315281575.

Rizzolatti, Giacomo. 2008. *Mirrors in the Brain: How Our Minds Share Actions and Emotions*. Edited by Corrado Sinigaglia. Oxford University Press.

Robinson, Shannon Marie. 2019. "Critical Design in Librarianship: Visual and Narrative Exploration for Critical Praxis." *Library Quarterly* 89, no. 4 (October): 348–61. https://doi.org/10.1086/704965.

Roshanaei, Mahnaz, Christopher Tran, Sylvia Morelli, Cornelia Caragea, and Elena Zheleva. 2019. "Paths to Empathy: Heterogeneous Effects of Reading Personal Stories Online." *Proceedings of the 2019 IEEE International Conference on Data Science and Advanced Analytics, DSAA 2019*, no. 1: 570–79. https://doi.org/10.1109/DSAA.2019.00072.

Slovic, Paul. 2007. "If I Look at the Mass I Will Never Act: Psychic Numbing and Genocide." *Judgment and Decision Making* 2 (February): 79–95. https://doi.org/10.1007/978-90-481-8647-1_3.

Sturm, Brian W. 1999. "The Enchanted Imagination: Storytelling's Power to Entrance Listeners." *School Library Media Research* 2: 1–21.

Sturm, Brian W., and Sarah Beth Nelson. 2016. "With Our Own Words: Librarians' Perceptions of the Values of Storytelling in Libraries." *Storytelling, Self, Society* 12, no. 1: 4–4. www.jstor.org/stable/10.13110/storselfsoci.12.1.0004.

Tuck, Eve, and K. Wayne Yang. 2012. "Decolonization Is Not a Metaphor." *Decolonization: Indigeneity, Education & Society* 1, no. 1 (September): 1–40. https://jps.library.utoronto.ca/index.php/des/article/view/18630.

Critical Storytelling

Understanding Storyteller, Audience, and Story Relationships

S o many of the best ideas come from the exchange of stories. Years ago, I was sitting around a table with other librarians as we discussed a building renovation project. We were all staring at draft blueprints and measurements of the basement rooms in every dimension, from square footage to ceiling height. We had a problem because the old concrete ceiling made it impossible to raise the room's height. All we could do was cover up the concrete grid that had hung over our heads all these years. But by covering it up, the ceiling would be even lower, and we knew the space would feel small no matter how large the footprint. As we stared at the data and talked it over, one of my colleagues had a brilliant insight. Why don't we dig the floor deeper? That's exactly what we did, and the basement of that library still feels light, airy, and open today.

This is a story about the ways that we are smarter together as colleagues. It is also a story about looking beyond the apparent limitations of the data in front of you. Most of all, it is a story about digging deeper. To become effective library advocacy storytellers—when making reports, writing newsletters, crafting presentations, or having casual conversations in the community—we need to dig deeper into the injustices that surround libraries as institutions and cultural spaces. Data—numbers, statistics, charts, graphs, visuals, interactive dashboards—alone can't tell the story.

This chapter explores the fundamentals of storytelling as a dynamic process of making meaning together. Sharing stories is the way that humans have always made community and experienced belonging, and sharing effective and compelling data stories requires a rich understanding of storytelling. However, storytelling will not do the critical work of advocating for equity and social justice without library data storytellers digging deeper into their own standpoints, positionality, and power.

The Storytelling Triangle

Storytelling happens in a dynamic relationship between three interacting elements, symbolized by the triangle in figure 1.1. First, there is the *teller*, whose job it is to take data and shape the story. Second, there is the *audience*, who are more than just listeners. They reshape and refine the story through their reactions as they listen. They also have the potential power to retell the story. Third is the *story* itself, which will be grounded in facts and evidence but can also engage and entertain.

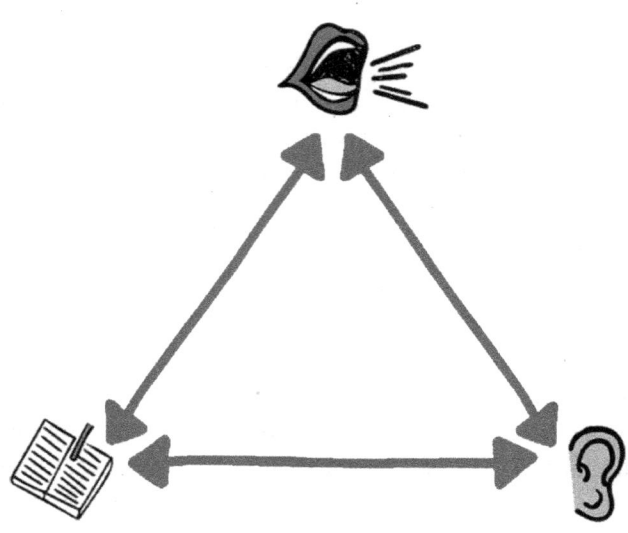

FIGURE 1.1
The storytelling triangle

Credit: Hilary Pope, www.linkedin.com/in/hilary-pope-a71a0116/

Each of the relationships in this triangle matters profoundly. The teller is always working with the audience, and each story will emerge in a particular form because of this symbiotic relationship. The relationships inform each other: The audience's relationship to the teller hinges in part on how they understand the teller's own relationship to the story, as well as which story the teller chooses to tell that audience.

Relationships of Trust in Storytelling ────────────

Trust Between Teller and Audience

First, for storytelling to occur, there must be a basic relationship of *trust between the teller and the audience.* This trust is contextual and multifaceted. It depends on demonstrating that the teller wants *this* audience to receive *this* story. The teller needs to know something about the audience, which is the first place where storytelling can go wrong. If the teller presumes to know an audience without having cultural knowledge or having done adequate research, they may not establish trust. Even worse are those moments when the teller is unaware of their ignorance about or biases toward groups whose identities—cultural, ethnic, religious, and more—are subjected to demeaning stereotypes, especially if those identities differ from the teller's own. Because of pervasive biases in society, the teller must unpack their own biases to avoid alienating the audience. In simple terms, this entails enacting cultural humility from the position of power as storyteller. From their book *Cultural Humility,* David Hurley et al. describe a way of being in libraries that should inform the teller's words, actions, and interactions with their audience:

> Rather than seek competence in interacting with people of other cultures, be open to cultural dynamics in any interaction. Let the other person determine how relevant their culture is to the interaction and be cognizant of the power imbalances. Be aware of and work to correct the structural inequities in your organization or profession, some of which come from inaccurate cultural assumptions. Understand the power imbalances present in interactions and practice critical self-reflection. (Hurley et al. 2022)

Cultural humility is the basis of critical respect for audiences. Respect is a precursor to the trust necessary for listening.

In professional contexts, trust is often relatively easy to establish, especially when the purpose of the story is clear and the teller and audience share common interests or values, such as sustaining libraries as institutions. When there is trust, the storytelling relationships between teller and audience can even be robust in virtual contexts (McDowell 2008). Cultivating trust with an audience is simple, but, depending on the context and history, it may not be easy. Honesty and openness are the basic precursors to trust, but factors like consistency and coherence also matter, especially in organizational storytelling. Organizational storytelling is about motivating the people who work in an organization with a story about action, values, a future vision, or a sense of belonging with a shared mission. "Narrative is the foundation of an organization's brand" (Denning 2011). In organizations, trust means that the leaders and members of an organization must align around a similar story internally. When communicating externally, they must behave in ways that align with the stories they tell. Histories—institutional, personal, and cultural—also matter when establishing trust between teller and audience.

The Teller's Relationship to the Story

Second, the *teller must understand their relationship to the story*. Story in data storytelling involves careful and explicit interpretation, and the teller is responsible for crafting and defending that interpretation. Storytellers are not neutral; they bring a point of view to the story that becomes inherent in the story as it is told. This is most obviously the case with a personal story, when the person who lived the story is telling it, but it also matters in stories about libraries and communities. For example, a front-line library staffer's relationship to the library is different than that of the director or a board member. The audience deserves to know how we came to know the story we are telling (see box 1.1).

At the same time, and perhaps paradoxically, the teller's understanding of their relationship to the story should not overshadow the story itself. It is tempting to talk too much about how we came to know what we know because, after all, this is part of the story of our lives. To recall that the purpose of LIS storytelling is not to aggrandize the teller may inform how much to say about your relationship to the story: "Remember, you are the instrument; the story is the main feature" (Bishop and Kimball 2006, 30). Succinctly communicating your relationship to the story helps your audience consider how they will relate to the story.

BOX 1.1

What Is Your Relationship to the Story?

The best way to think about your relationship to the story is to ask how you came to know this story. Possible answers that are not mutually exclusive include:

- a research process of gathering and analyzing data
- a research process of searching for published analyses
- everyday lived experience
- listening to the story of another person or group of people
- data collected automatically by a computer system
- community survey data
- library staff survey data
- observational data collected systematically
- community input
- committee or board work

There is no right or wrong answer to how you came to know your story, just as there is no objectively better or worse relationship we have to data. But in a particular context, it might be more compelling to an audience to understand that, for example, your story is based on both everyday lived experience and data rather than on experience alone. How we know what we know matters to audiences and impacts the persuasiveness of our stories.

The Audience's Relationship to the Story

Third, the *audience has a relationship to the story*. Everything the teller says, writes, and presents informs that relationship. For example, if the story is about the importance of sustaining and increasing the use of a service that has grown less popular over time, audience members will relate to that story differently if they receive ongoing benefits from that service, if they used it in the past but stopped using it, or if they have never heard of this service. They will also relate to the story differently, for example, if the service saves them or their household money or if they can afford to purchase something similar on their own—the power of income matters.

Similarly, from a critical respect for audience standpoint, the backgrounds of audience members will impact how they hear a story about, for example, library connections to local food and shelter relief agencies. An audience member receiving food stamps will understand the need for keeping those connections robust in a different way than an individual unfamiliar with or judgmental of such programs.

The storyteller may or may not know whether those in the audience have such experiences (or biases). Further, audience members may or may not choose to share such information based on a wide array of factors, including their sense of centrality or marginalization relative to others in attendance. A person who feels centered in a group is more likely to be confident in disclosing past experiences; one who feels marginalized or even stigmatized is less likely to do so. Recalling that every audience represents a wider array of human experience than the teller can ever know is a necessary exercise in compassion and humility and a good reminder that audiences have their own relationships to stories. Not knowing what the audience will make of a story is a simple fact of storytelling (see box 1.2).

BOX 1.2
Rehearsal Audiences

It is difficult to predict what meaning audiences will make of stories, but it is not impossible to gather some experiential data to refine and hone the message of a library advocacy story. Rehearsal audiences will hear your story and then tell back what they heard. Such audiences may be colleagues in your library, from another library, or in another profession that involves advocacy, such as nonprofit education. They may also be loyal patrons, customers, or donors who have a vested interest in impactful library storytelling. Rehearsal audiences can even be friendly critics who are willing to "kick the tires" on a nearly completed story. Completion, in this case, means you have completed data collection and analysis and are considering how to communicate the findings. The following table explores some of the dimensions of story development and how they align with strategies for choosing effective rehearsal audiences.

Story Development with Rehearsal Audience

Percentage of Story Complete	Stage of Story Development	Recommended Rehearsal Audience
Up to 30% developed	Early stage: still bringing focus to the data presentation and considering story strategies	Very friendly audiences: allies who already understand your ideas and support your mission
30–80% developed	Middle stage: clear data and clear ideas for story strategies but not sure what audiences are likely to remember	Friendly audiences who can take the perspective of prospective audiences, such as funders, and offer supportive input
Over 80% developed	Final stage: data and story are fully developed and almost ready to present to target audiences	Friendly and critical audiences who can refine the details of the story and visuals

The crucial part is this: *Before* asking for feedback, *ask the rehearsal audience to tell you what they heard.* Either ask them to tell the story back to you, or identify the main message of your data story. Listen carefully to what they say. If it wasn't what you hoped they would take away, then your next steps to refine the story and visuals are often clear. If they are unclear, discuss what you hoped for and how the story can be improved.

Storytelling can be profoundly and even poetically collective and a shared experience of story can lead to synchronized responses—laughter, sighing, knowing nods, intense stillness—that contribute both experientially and cognitively to the audience's understanding of the story. The audience's relationship to the story will determine their questions about the story, what they believe about the story, and how likely they are to retell it to others.

As storytellers, one way to practice and cultivate humility about the audience's relationship to the story is to remain calm and focused enough to listen carefully.

Sometimes it is possible to feel how the audience collectively relates to the story simply by listening, watching facial expressions, and observing body language. Even though individuals will still take away their own version of the story, this form of listening can provide important insights (more on this in chapter 4).

Humility in relation to story, audience, and the storyteller's role is easier to understand and practice when we connect this to broader critical concepts of cultural humility, which are in turn grounded in cultural competence.

Cultural Competence and Storytelling

Defining Cultural Competence

When there is established trust between the storyteller and the audience, cultural competence permeates that trust. It is the bedrock of the ideal connection between teller and audience:

> Cultural competence is the ability to recognize the significance of culture in one's own life and in the lives of others; and to come to know and respect diverse cultural backgrounds and characteristics through interaction with individuals from diverse linguistic, cultural, and socioeconomic groups; and to fully integrate the culture of diverse groups into services, work, and institutions in order to enhance the lives of both those being served by the library profession and those engaged in service. (Montiel Overall 2009, 189–90)

In storytelling, cultural competence respects how the audience's lived experiences, cultures, and positionalities differ from the storyteller's own. Cultural competence should also inform decisions about whose stories it is right or wrong for me to tell—more on this in chapter 3.

Library data storytelling requires significant cultural competence to see real people represented by data. Numbers and percentages often represent real people in diverse communities, sometimes fairly and sometimes in biased ways. Cultural competence in this kind of work means seeing how data about people's everyday information needs—job applications, navigating social services, finding community—relates directly to social needs and social inequities—income disparities, housing prices, food availability or deserts, health care, and more.

Although a diversity workshop may result in a certificate of training, cultural competence is an ongoing growth and learning process. Nicole A. Cooke (2016) defines cultural competence as a spectrum, from incompetent to proficient, demonstrating that cultural competence cannot be a one-time achievement. With work, we move further toward proficiency. With neglect, however, we backslide into the everyday biases of the status quo.

Connecting Cultural Competence with Social Justice

Cultural competence is a practiced skill, but the ways professionals implement it necessarily interconnect with other values like equity and social justice. And yet, what a library worker must do to embrace both cultural competence and social justice is complex and contextual. For example, in their chapter in the 2022 book *Social Justice Design and Implementation in Library and Information Science*, Julie Nichols et al. explore cooking as a metaphor for design processes. Among the "cooking implements" are "cultural awareness and sensitive engagement, active listening, growth mindset, concept-driven thinking, collage ideas, storyboarding, engagement with reading materials, and precedents" (Nichols et al. 2022, 147). These skills are contextual and are often used in dynamic moment-to-moment ways that can ultimately build or damage trust. In the long term, enacting these skills of cultural competence leads to greater social justice.

Social justice in libraries and LIS has a long and imperfect history. In their powerful book on this topic, Nicole A. Cooke and Miriam E. Sweeney (2017) describe the complexity of the term *social justice* and the ways that library workers, librarians, and LIS scholars may interchangeably use terms such as *human rights*, *ethics*, *diversity*, and *inclusion*, covering a vast range of topics in the field (33–36). They propose a set of clear values as a universal social justice stance for LIS curricula:

1. All humans have an inherent worth and deserve information services that help address their needs.
2. People perceive reality and information in different ways, and in different contexts. This needs to be acknowledged.
3. There are many different types of information and knowledge, and these are societal resources.
4. LIS theory, practice, research, and professional preparation are pursued with the ultimate goal of bringing positive change to service constituencies.
5. The provision of information is an inherently powerful activity. Distributing information is, in itself, a political act. (Cooke and Sweeney 2017, 36–40)

In this sense, data storytelling is a specific kind of information provision that, like all distribution of information, we must view as a political act, especially when the intent is to serve citizens as a well-informed electorate that participates in and sustains democracy.

Critical Approaches to Storytelling

Who tells the library's stories? Critical approaches to storytelling include assessments of the typical storytellers. Library leaders, for example, are expected to tell library data stories, although everyone in a library may have a point of view to share, from workers to patrons. Consideration of whose voices are included and systemically excluded from discourse is an important step in reflecting on what data stories capture and what they leave out (Cooke and Kitzie 2021; Mehra 2021). When systemic injustices lead to the discriminatory exclusion of people's points of view, scholars argue for counter-narratives, leveraging tools like autoethnography from storytellers whose perspectives are too often dismissed (Cooke 2019; Patin et al. 2021a; Patin et al. 2021b; McDowell et al. 2021). The LIS field routinely limits voices by treating people only as "users" when instead they could be framed as "knowers, speakers, listeners, . . . informants" (Oliphant 2021, 951), and storytellers. The analysis of storytelling in information classrooms—in LIS and other information degree programs—reveals patterns of "calling out injustice" and "calling in the audience" that reflect students' social justice storytelling and demonstrate the ability to engage and provoke audiences to take action (McDowell and Cooke 2022). Empowering future librarians as critical storytellers means provoking a sea change in whose voices are heard and understood as important.

Defining "Critical"

Central to critical theory is questioning power—who holds power, who benefits from it, and who is excluded from it. As mentioned in the introduction, critical theory has its roots in the Frankfurt School philosophers who argued for explicit understandings of power and the systemic forces of oppression that prevent human liberation (Arato and Gebhardt 1982). They wrote in response to the existential crisis of the Nazi takeover of much of Europe in the late 1930s and early 1940s, a wave of fascism that caused millions of human deaths at the hands of a machine-like state. They saw threats in the forms of the industrialization of culture (Marcuse 1964), mass media and conformity in the arts and music (Adorno 2006), and the mechanical duplication of everyday objects that had previously been handmade (Benjamin 2008). They drew on Marxist thought in spirit, although not in political prescription, to question or critique hegemony, meaning, and cultural forms of power that led to human oppression. They particularly questioned state systems that stole life and liberty from citizens systematically, and often silently. By 1940 many of these philosophers had fled Europe for the freedom of thought available in the United States. Among them were the leading philosophical proponents of modern democratization movements, who promoted communication as an act of political freedom (Habermas 1989).

Critical race theory is a second branch of the term *critical.* It is based in legal scholarship that, similarly, argues for human liberation by revealing political and economic injustices that are racist and ubiquitous, codified into law as "justice" and yet systemically unjust (Crenshaw 1989). While civil rights grew in the United States in the 1960s with equity in education and voting, those gains have been eroded with new forms of inequity that, for example, create new obstacles to voting that disproportionately impact people with less money. Civil rights lawyers and legal scholars have argued for an understanding of racism as hegemonic, culturally ubiquitous, and invisible or minimized. The disproportionate number of Black people in prisons, for example, aligns strikingly with the number of Black people who were enslaved in the nineteenth century and were subject to racist Jim Crow laws in the twentieth century (Alexander 2010, 290). Hegemonic racist culture purports to give everyone equal opportunities, ignoring data that demonstrates that inequities are real and systemic. American law has historically supported fewer rights, less wealth, property, and as a result less dignity for non-white citizens when compared with white citizens (Bell 1973). Controversy over the term *critical* is difficult because to avoid thinking about power is, in the case of dominant cultural groups, to benefit from that power unconsciously.

Critical in this context means a way of thinking that seeks to see power, understand inequality, and create greater equity. Critical thought assumes that the inequities which data shows to be systematic are not the fault of individuals, but instead have systemic causes. Critical data means seeing patterns in numbers and questioning stereotypes of individuals or groups that blame people for having less power. Critical storytelling asks questions about social justice, cultural competence, and what stories will make the world more just and equitable. Critical data storytelling requires looking at patterns of inequity while also imagining beyond them, so that library data stories are told in service of making libraries places that seek, support, and sustain human liberation.

Inclusion and Social Justice

Critical approaches to storytelling also require questioning stories themselves and how their content relates to social justice goals. Lee Anne Bell (2010) defines storytelling as social justice by classifying stories told about race and racism—stock, concealed, resistance, and emerging/transforming stories—at different points on the path toward justice. Unfortunately, there is evidence that critical approaches routinely fall short of their promise in actual workplace outcomes. Performativity, or the desire to seem unbiased, often overrides a genuine commitment to examining the ways that our own biases prevent full inclusion and equity. This examination must be culturally humble and align internal insights with actions that make a difference. To seem or perform as unbiased without deeper critical reflection and considered action "is to be an active participant in structural inequity" (Ferretti 2020). Performativity is a perennial concern; since stories emerge between teller and audience, the audience's reactions may shape the story and diminish or even co-opt challenging information, thus maintaining the status quo. Without a critical mindset that considers who has power and who is left out, storytelling has frequently simply repeated stories of exclusion.

Cultural competence in LIS, however, elevates cultural knowledge in any form—practices, stories, customs, jokes, and more—as relevant to information seekers as whole people. There are parallels to storytelling in the process of developing cultural competence:

> Developing cultural competence is a dialectical process in which individuals examine their own mental representation of the world along with the mental representations of others. Adjustments in preconceptions about others' culture result in a readjustment of the place of culture in society. Cultural competence is the ability to make the adjustment and to participate in making culture an important part of the ethos of an organization. (Montiel Overall 2009)

Ideally, storytelling and listening are part of an ongoing cycle of communication, relationship-building, and understanding. In this sense, and with a critical mindset that puts the library values of inclusion and access into action through listening, storytelling can be a powerful tool for developing and sustaining individual and organizational cultural competence.

But even when a library is thoroughly committed to listening in a dynamic storytelling exchange, all audiences may not agree. Subsets of communities may conflict with other subsets, and people in dominant groups may use power to silence stories from those people who are less powerful. This potential for conflict makes critical approaches to audiences one of the most complex aspects of critical data storytelling. Before considering critical approaches to audiences, it is necessary to introduce one further concept: counter-storytelling.

The Need for Counter-Storytelling in LIS

Counter-storytelling means telling the stories that push back against systemic inequities and biases. As Cooke (2016) argues in her work redefining diversity in LIS, "It is hard work teaching about racism, social justice, and other topics, especially in LIS, which is characteristically known as a white and female field, and it is even harder to teach these topics when I am typically the only person of color in the classroom" (322). Hence, for counter-storytelling in LIS to disrupt patterns of exclusion and bias, LIS professionals must actively listen to hear excluded stories.

In data storytelling, counter-storytelling means being cautious about excluding some data results as outliers. We must understand that when data points represent people or their lived experiences, the patterns in the data may also reflect and reiterate inequities in society. Outliers, meaning data points that don't fit larger patterns, could reflect the reality that dominant groups have certain kinds of power while people whose lives don't fit the mainstream have less. Outliers may contain the most important information for enacting justice.

Counter-storytelling with data requires an awareness of the contexts—including inequities and injustices—that impact the communities that libraries serve and the allocation of library resources, from services to data collection. This requires looking beyond routine questions to discover what the dominant patterns in data can obscure, which data is not collected, and whose experiences are not counted.

The Insider-Outsider Dynamic and Whiteness in LIS

Diversity of audiences is a good and powerful thing, and yet, in most if not all human societies, the insider-outsider dynamic allows some groups to dominate while silencing others. Because normative whiteness in librarianship has been so profound and difficult to uproot, this dynamic must be a central part of conversations about respect.

The LIS field avoided the issue of race for many years; by centering "race as the primary axis of analysis in the reinterpretation of major theoretical issues in LIS," Todd Honma (2005, 1) asks questions (and invites stories) that would not be possible with ignorance of race as a social construct. Other research shows that the term *multicultural* is used to sidestep the unequal legacies of race across multiple models in LIS. As Christine Pawley notes, "Practitioners and library users, too, embody diverse experiences and knowledge—if only we can find a way to take advantage of these" (2006, 165). Without critical approaches, libraries will continue to default to implicitly centering some people, usually white people, and ignoring others.

The Culturally Humble Storyteller

As Cooke writes, cultural humility is a "challenge to recognize the power dynamics and imbalances that exist between service providers and those receiving services. Cultural humility also challenges practitioners to rectify these power imbalances whenever possible, especially in regard to race, ethnicity, class, linguistic ability, and sexual orientation" (Cooke 2017, 20). In data storytelling, there is no telling without listening, which the teller cannot force upon the audience without damaging the trust that constitutes the storytelling triangle. Coming from a place of humility, the teller must remember in live oral storytelling that they cannot control the audience and the story. Channeling cultural humility and respecting the power dynamics in data storytelling make for a meaningful, memorable story: "The circumstance that forces you to be humble is also what makes it so miraculous when you succeed" (Lipman 1999, 18).

Humility on the part of the storyteller is central to the LIS storytelling tradition, where librarians have been in service to their listeners. It is also relevant to any storytelling situation because the storyteller must accept that the audience will make meaning from each story they hear. Stories that last through multiple retellings are created and re-created with audiences, not just presented to them. This co-creation means audiences not only interpret stories, but they also deserve the opportunity to change roles and take up the role of storyteller.

And yet library workers have not consistently adopted cultural humility. According to Jennifer Ferretti, "While critical pedagogy in librarianship has changed the way we teach information literacy and think of the teacher/student relationship," it has "been slower to change power relations between library colleagues" (2020, 134). The difficulty in understanding when power is unevenly distributed in the library is indicative of a lack of cultural humility that makes it difficult for professionals to enact equity among coworkers. The defensiveness of those who benefit from having more power in the library can obscure those moments when counter-storytelling is necessary.

Data cannot explain what causes inequities. The data can only reveal the problems. For example, research assessing trends in National Institutes of Health (NIH) grant funding shows a strong correlation between applicants' race and ethnicity and the funding awarded to them: White applicants routinely receive funding in higher amounts than people of color (Ginther et al. 2011). The data stories based on this information can spark valuable conversations about dismantling systemic racism in higher education, including in medical libraries and LIS programs where health informatics researchers may receive NIH funds.

Data storytelling for libraries requires a direct and explicit engagement with race and power so that diversity is more than a slogan, a performative tolerance, or a shallow celebration. An ethics of inclusion as part of data storytelling would look for data outliers and listen to unheard voices. For example, imagine a community whose demographics have changed over the years, with small but rapidly increasing numbers of citizens who speak languages other than English. This demographic data can be critical to assessing and improving library services and collections across language abilities in the community (see Box 1.3). In an era of unprecedented white supremacist maneuvering in the United States, however, an appreciation of human rights and dignity must inform library advocacy storytelling and the use of demographic data to avoid unintentional discrimination. Storytelling must not merely placate groups or accommodate beliefs that have no basis in fact or data.

With a foundation of cultural humility, library data storytelling can serve people equitably in communities. There is the potential for library data storytelling to contribute emerging/transforming stories toward greater social justice (Bell 2010). Tellers must commit to listening to their audiences—the people in the communities they serve—in a way that intertwines cultural competence, cultural humility, social justice, and an overall understanding that data can provide a road map to greater equity.

> **BOX 1.3**
> *Citizenship and Library Data*
>
> In a conversation about how to make library data available to anyone, a group of experts encountered a dilemma. Should they include data about people in the United States—citizenship status, country of birth, languages spoken at home? In a federal environment of incomplete and confusing immigration laws and regulations, how could they prevent this data from targeting or harming people in specific communities?
>
> These questions have many implications. Taxpaying non-citizens support and have the right to use the full services of public libraries. Knowing which languages are spoken at home can be valuable for considering how to fully serve people in communities. At the same time, there has been rampant hatred in the United States related to exactly these questions of who "belongs" and who is "other."
>
> As people committed to library ideals, the experts did not want data to lead to further suffering. The deciding factor was the role of the library in communities. Libraries frequently host citizenship classes, especially in urban areas. Libraries need to know who in their community could benefit from such services, so they decided to make the data available but left a note about their concerns in the project documentation.

Audience Respect

In data storytelling, respect is multifaceted. It includes the storyteller taking responsibility for providing context with data so the audience clearly sees how the data was collected and interpreted. This gesture respects the audience's right to know the context of a data story and the storyteller's method(s) of analysis and interpretation.

Audiences are comprised of individuals, each of whom may have their own interpretation of a story. What sets storytelling apart from other communication methods is the basic assumption of audience interpretation: A story will not travel just as it was told, but will change over time through different tellers and different retellings to different audiences.

Audiences are also groups, and group dynamics matter in live situations like board meetings, faculty meetings, or city council chambers. Even in, and perhaps especially in, such situations, the individual members of such political bodies are empowered to interpret what they hear in different ways. In this case, each member of the audience must make their own decision about how to cast a vote. Understanding that groups can have strong commonalities and yet be comprised of fully independent individuals is key to creating a respectful relationship with any audience.

It can be tempting to believe that stories exist in data, but they do not. Stories are always constructed by a process of human interpretation. This means that storytellers bear a special responsibility to explain their interpretations and to allow for the possibility that audiences might add to understandings of data. Acknowledging that the storyteller's role includes interpretation demonstrates respect for the audience. A deeper dive into audience dynamics in these contentious and polarized times is provided in chapter 4.

Storytellers must become listeners to empower audiences to take up telling. They must acknowledge audiences as part of the story-making process, not as afterthoughts, receptacles, or "markets." Audiences must know that they are part of the story, giving reactions and feedback that change how the story is told. If audience members can react to library data stories by sharing their own interpretations and experiences and become storytellers themselves, the story that emerges in that dynamic storytelling exchange may be a better story.

Co-Created and Emergent Stories

Storytelling is especially amenable to critical approaches because the audience has the power to interpret. The co-creation and emergent aspects of storytelling require seeing the audience's power to interpret and retell stories. Any story that is retold, spontaneously, by those who have heard it signals a very different kind of power than an official story.

Wisdom and storytelling have long been associated, in part because story allows for the accumulation of wisdom, with the audience acting as editor (McDowell et al. 2021). If wisdom is carried by stories and accumulates in them as they are retold, then wisdom could be defined as an emergent quality of the storytelling dynamic between teller and audience. Recent global crises have engendered bias in many forms, including epistemicide or "the killing, silencing, annihilation, or devaluing of a way of knowing" (Patin et al. 2021b, 1306). Resisting this annihilation of knowledge by listening, in the moment and in the systematic gathering and re-sharing of stories, is a critical move toward greater wisdom for libraries as organizations. Just as knowledge need not be the attribute of one individual knower, storytelling and the story that emerges can belong to groups, institutions, and even cultures. Being a storyteller is an action in context, not a characteristic, and many narrators are needed to enrich effective library data storytelling.

Storytelling and a commitment to understanding knowledge as comprised of many narratives would mean that the study of information would be more epistemologically diverse. For example, it would open space for practices of learning that are "built upon the perspectives of Native peoples while incorporating compatible key values of LIS" while taking critical approaches to resist re-creating "colonial models of information gathering, organizing, and sharing" (Roy 2015, 384, 408). But just as Indigenous ideas are frequently destroyed in their manner of adoption (or adaptation, or co-optation), changing the roles of storyteller and audience alone will not solve structural inequities, biases, or power differentials, either in society or in libraries. For example, between young adults and adults, changing roles does not create equality and "to disavow or deny such power differentials would rapidly erode trust" (McDowell 2020, 106). The triangle of teller, listener, and story is never static, and while storytelling with humility means looking for opportunities to listen, those opportunities are merely the starting point for structural change and greater social equity.

Conclusion: Storytelling as Power

Ultimately, a story's power lies in the hands of the teller's abilities and the audience's hearing and remembering. The data storyteller has the power to tell and to persuade and the responsibility to remain honest. The audience has the power to listen and to connect or disconnect. This dynamic process allows more profound exchanges between libraries and the communities they serve. Deeper connections are forged when storytellers become listeners and invite listeners to become storytellers. Centering story and storytelling challenges us to include a richer variety of stories, tellers, and audiences whose dynamic exchanges will inform a more inclusive future.

Critical approaches to storytelling are necessary because, no matter how we have embraced ideas of equity, diversity, and inclusion in library services, we are not where we should be. Libraries routinely regress to lower levels of institutional cultural competence, to the assumption that a community's stories are already heard and known, and to an uneasy ignorance of the bias and injustices around and in libraries. In other words, libraries routinely regress to the status quo.

And so we need to dig deeper. Storytelling requires us to consider data as meaningful so it can be told in story form. It requires thoughtful consideration of power and of audiences. By seeking community stories as fervently as we seek information, the world of libraries could radically and inclusively transform not only where but also how and why we seek information. Hearing people's stories not only as culturally and emotionally relevant but also as informationally relevant challenges libraries to make visible the places where we need more stories. As a field, we must dig into practices like storytelling to confront the limits of how things have always been done.

REFERENCES

Adorno, Theodor W., with Rolf Tiedemann. 2006. *History and Freedom: Lectures 1964-1965*. Polity.

Alexander, Michelle. 2010. *The New Jim Crow: Mass Incarceration in the Age of Colorblindness*. New Press.

Arato, Andrew, and Eike Gebhardt. 1982. *The Essential Frankfurt School Reader*. Continuum.

Bell, Derrick. 1973. *Race, Racism, and American Law*. Little, Brown.

Bell, Lee Anne. 2010. *Storytelling for Social Justice: Connecting Narrative and the Arts in Antiracist Teaching*. 2nd edition. Routledge. https://doi .org/10.4324/9780203852231.

Benjamin, Walter. 2008. *The Work of Art in the Age of Mechanical Reproduction*. Translated by J. A. Underwood. Penguin Books.

Bishop, Kay, and Melanie A. Kimball. 2006. "Engaging Students in Storytelling." *Teacher Librarian* 33, no. 4: 28-31.

Cooke, Nicole A. 2016. "Developing Cultural Competence." In *Information Services to Diverse Populations: Developing Culturally Competent Library Professionals*, 19-30. Libraries Unlimited.

Cooke, Nicole A. 2017. *Information Services to Diverse Populations: Developing Culturally Competent Library Professionals*. Libraries Unlimited.

Cooke, Nicole A. 2019. "Impolite Hostilities and Vague Sympathies: Academia as a Site of Cyclical Abuse." *Journal of Education for Library and Information Science* 60, no. 3: 223-30. https://doi.org/10.3138/jelis.2019-0005.

Cooke, Nicole A., and Vanessa L. Kitzie. 2021. "Outsiders-within-Library and Information Science: Reprioritizing the Marginalized in Critical Sociocultural Work." *Journal of the Association for Information Science and Technology* 72, no. 10: 1285-94. https://doi.org/10.1002/asi.24449.

Cooke, Nicole A., and Miriam E. Sweeney. 2017. *Teaching for Justice: Implementing Social Justice in the LIS Classroom.* Library Juice.

Crenshaw, Kimberle. 1989. "Demarginalizing the Intersection of Race and Sex: A Black Feminist Critique of Antidiscrimination Doctrine, Feminist Theory and Antiracist Politics." *University of Chicago Legal Forum*, no. 1. https://chicagounbound.uchicago.edu/uclf/vol1989/iss1/8.

Denning, Stephen. 2011. *The Leader's Guide to Storytelling: Mastering the Art and Discipline of Business Narrative.* Revised and updated edition. Jossey-Bass.

Ferretti, Jennifer A. 2020. "Building a Critical Culture: How Critical Librarianship Falls Short in the Workplace." *Communications in Information Literacy* 14, no. 1. https://doi.org/10.15760/comminfolit.2020.14.1.10.

Ginther, Donna K., Walter T. Schaffer, Joshua Schnell, Beth Masimore, Faye Liu, Laurel L. Haak, and Raynard Kington. 2011. "Race, Ethnicity, and NIH Research Awards." *Science* 333, no. 6045: 1015-19. https://doi.org/10.1126/science.1196783.

Habermas, Jürgen. 1989. *The Structural Transformation of the Public Sphere: An Inquiry into a Category of Bourgeois Society.* Translated by Thomas Burger. MIT Press.

Honma, Todd. 2005. "Trippin' Over the Color Line: The Invisibility of Race in Library and Information Studies." *InterActions: UCLA Journal of Education and Information Studies* 1, no. 2. https://doi.org/10.5070/D412000540.

Hurley, David A., Sarah R. Kostelecky, and Lori Townsend. 2022. *Cultural Humility.* American Library Association.

Lipman, Doug. 1999. *Improving Your Storytelling: Beyond the Basics for All Who Tell Stories in Work or Play.* August House.

Marcuse, Herbert. 1964. *One-Dimensional Man: Studies in the Ideology of Advanced Industrial Society.* Beacon.

McDowell, Kate. 2008. "Distance and Presence: A Case Study of Performance in Two Online Storytelling Library Resources." *Storytelling, Self, Society* 4, no. 3: 214-34.

McDowell, Kate. 2020. "Storytelling, Young Adults, and Three Paradoxes." In *Transforming Young Adult Services,* 2nd ed., edited by Anthony Bernier. ALA Neal-Schuman.

McDowell, Kate, and Nicole A. Cooke. 2022. "Social Justice Storytelling: A Pedagogical Imperative." *The Library Quarterly* 92, no. 4 (October): 355–78. https://doi.org/10.1086/721391.

McDowell, Kate, Nicole Cooke, Janice Del Negro, Beth Patin, and Curtis Tenney. 2021. "Storytelling and/as Resilience." "Proceedings of the Association for Library and Information Science Annual Conference 2021." September 20. Association for Library and Information Science Education. https://hdl.handle.net/2142/110953.

Mehra, Bharat. 2021. *Social Justice Design and Implementation in Library and Information Science.* Routledge.

Montiel Overall, Patricia. 2009. "Cultural Competence: A Conceptual Framework for Library and Information Science Professionals." *Library Quarterly* 79, no. 2: 175–204. Library & Information Science Source. www.journals.uchicago.edu/doi/10.1086/597080.

Nichols, Julie, Jia Tina Du, Stefan Peters, Darren Fong, Angelica Harris-Faull, Ning Gu, Anna Leditschke, and Jannatul Fardous. 2022. "Conceptualizing Co-Mapping Knowledges to Promote Social Justice Outcomes with Aboriginal Communities through Design Pedagogy." In *Social Justice Design and Implementation in Library and Information Science,* edited by Bharat Mehra. Routledge.

Oliphant, Tami. 2021. "Emerging (Information) Realities and Epistemic Injustice." *Journal of the Association for Information Science and Technology* 72, no. 8: 951–62. https://doi.org/10.1002/asi.24461.

Patin, Beth, Tami Oliphant, Danielle Allard, LaVerne Gray, Rachel Ivy Clarke, Jasmina Tacheva, and Kayla Lar-Son. 2021a. "At the Margins of Epistemology: Amplifying Alternative Ways of Knowing in Library and Information Science." *Proceedings of the Association for Information Science & Technology* 58, no. 1: 630–33. https://doi.org/10.1002/pra2 515.

Patin, Beth, Melinda Sebastian, Jieun Yeon, Danielle Bertolini, and Alexandra Grimm. 2021b. "Interrupting Epistemicide: A Practical Framework for Naming, Identifying, and Ending Epistemic Injustice in the Information Professions." *Journal of the Association for Information Science and Technology* 72, no. 10: 1306–18. https://doi.org/10.1002/asi.24479.

Pawley, Christine. 2006. "Unequal Legacies: Race and Multiculturalism in the LIS Curriculum." *Library Quarterly* 76, no. 2: 149–68. Scopus. https://doi.org/10.1086/506955.

Roy, Loriene. 2015. "Advancing an Indigenous Ecology within LIS Education." *Library Trends* 64, no. 2: 384–414.

From Data to Story
Reframing the Library Data Collection Process

2

S ince 2020, in workshops with over 1,000 total participants from library-related fields, I have been asking for a show of hands or poll response to one question: "With which of the following are you most comfortable?"

1. Data
2. Story
3. Both
4. Neither

Most people choose either data or story, not both or neither. Over the last couple of years, I've watched an increasing number of people indicate that they are comfortable with both, but this still remains less than one-third of respondents. To investigate this further, our research team conducted a survey of thirty-nine library workers at all levels, from front-line staff to directors, and presented a summary of our findings in the form of two personas—story experts and data experts—as shown in table 2.1.

We may not always think of story as a kind of expertise. Even though we are all storytellers, there are those who have extraordinary talent or develop exceptional abilities to tell stories. Library staff are often drawn to this area of work because of a passion for narrative (reading, movies, gaming, etc.), and many former librarians have gone on to prominence in the US National Storytelling Festival (National Storytelling Network, n.d.). Those who work with children

TABLE 2.1
Developing Library Data Storytelling Personas

STORY EXPERTS	DATA EXPERTS
• Strong narrative skills • Strongly positive attitudes toward storytelling, mostly positive attitudes toward data with some aversion • Concerned about lack of data literacy and privacy/surveillance	• Strong data skills • Positive attitudes toward data and storytelling, but sometimes lack administrative support for storytelling • Concerned about composing narratives from analyses

(McDowell et al. 2024)

become experts at bringing stories alive for all-ages audiences, whether reading aloud or performing as a storyteller with a fully realized adaptation of, for example, a classic folktale. Data collection and analysis, on the other hand, is usually thought of as requiring expertise. More libraries, if they can afford it, have hired staff with data training and experience in recent years. Library staff have sought and found training from sources like Project Outcome, the Research Institute for Public Libraries, and the Association of College and Research Libraries. Data skills range widely, from understanding the capabilities of Excel to developing dashboards using more sophisticated data visualization software such as Tableau and Power BI.

Put simply, we are a bifurcated group of professionals, with strong expertise in either story or data, but most people are not experts in both. Framed as an opportunity, library data storytelling has the potential to bring people who are data experts together with story experts to synthesize new ways of working that will bridge internal divides to tell library data stories more powerfully.

Data Ownership and Anxiety

Even when there is no control over the data or the questions used to collect it, it's still possible to take control over the story. Recently, I worked with a library in Scandinavia that had a new data visualization software package, which could be used to create beautiful visual representations of trends, from program attendance to loan renewals. I pointed out a few trends that we could discuss, but the room remained quiet. "This is your data," I said. "What stories do you want to tell about it?" One participant spoke up and said it didn't feel like it was their data. "We don't choose what questions to ask," she said. "We have to collect this data for our government report."

Does library data feel like our data? We typically collect data for outside audiences, as part of following regulations that are routine and very important—data that can sometimes affect resource availability or the existence of the library itself. In many cases, data determines funding, staffing levels, service hours, and much more. Many of these determinations are made based on standardized data collection requirements that are usually imposed from the top down, by governmental agencies or legislative bodies that use this data to make comparisons between libraries and among different types of organizations. Library data reflects hard work and showcase achievements, but it can also be used to regulate libraries and other organizations right out of existence.

For many library workers and leaders, it is no wonder that data is sometimes a source of anxiety. Library staff, especially those who have negative attitudes toward data, can learn how to approach standard library data sets and visualizations with curiosity and creativity to overcome this anxiety. A storytelling mindset can open opportunities for seeing data as rooted in the everyday experiences of real people whose libraries deserve advocacy. So much time, energy, and staff work go into generating required reports, and yet we rarely have time to step back and look at the data as evidence that might inform an inspiring data story. Library data experts already know that storytelling can easily start from data collected and analyzed.

By considering the dynamic storytelling triangle and relationships at the outset, library staff can align library data collection processes with storytelling. This alignment means that library data has a full life cycle—not just visualization for a specific report or publication, but for communication to all stakeholders: library workers, leaders, and governing groups.

Library Data and Storytelling

The term *critical*, in this book, means a way of thinking that seeks to see power. Accepting that the power to interpret data is fully in our hands is a key first step. Data does not tell stories. Data also does not drive or decide. Those are human activities that require analysis and interpretation, which in turn require hard work of discernment and judgment rooted in professional ethics. Data can provide amazing insights, sobering realities, facts, trends, talking points, and more. Data can be the basis of some of the most powerful stories we create to explain why and how libraries matter. For an individual library, data can provide evidence for the current return on investment (ROI), or it can be useful for advocating for new forms of investments. Data is the evidence that can convince, but it is also the reality that must be contended with.

However, data is not neutral. It depends on how it is collected, so data is only as accurate and ethical as the systems used to capture the data. This becomes particularly important when we consider how often data, constructed in the interlocking societal context of patriarchy, racism, and other injustices, has overridden perspectives of people whose voices are routinely excluded from data collection processes. Data is only as fair as the people who collect and analyze it. Similarly, stories do not corrupt data. Stories do not lead to fantasy or fabrication. People make those choices and mistakes.

Libraries are astoundingly accomplished at collecting, and they deploy some of the most sophisticated methods for organizing collections and making them accessible. However, the practice of library collection is not the same as data collection. Data is not accessed by users in the same ways as other resources. Data must be brought to life as stories for library stakeholders—from decision-makers to the public—before it is put into storage like a collection. In other words, data needs a story before storage.

Data stories are not just sequences of events, just as stories are not merely beginning-middle-end, or else the most mundane lists would be great stories. Before constructing the sequence or chronology of a data story, it is important to organize the evidence and analysis with an underlying logic. This organizational approach is familiar to the logical structures of character, setting, and plot in stories. To be effective, data storytelling needs a structured story, which is built on clear evidence. This evidence can be the basis for a story that features classic library goals and motivations.[1]

Goals and Motivations

Great data stories for libraries are built on goals and motivations. The goals are based on data, and the motivations are based on the hopes for the story's message. Fortunately, there are a small number of common goals and motivations that underlie the ways that most library data stories are told, but we are not always aware of them. Understanding typical motivations for library data storytelling—and using data as evidence in story—clarifies intentions and supports the process of creating compelling stories out of the data collected.

Imagine a survey that reveals technology needs and those needs becoming a part of next year's budget. This budgetary wrangling happens so routinely that we often fail to tell the story about this work, but it is worth telling! Emory University recently conducted a survey, updated their technology, and shared a news story about this success: "We have analyzed results from a patron survey and have changed our investments in technology. We are ready to showcase the new computer workstations, laptops, and other equipment ready for checkout" (Emory Libraries 2023).

The underlying logic is so clear to insiders, but it is somewhat understated in the statement itself. In this case, the goal was to understand real needs, based on data, and then serve those needs. The motivation for the story was to share this achievement.

Goals

The logic behind a data story requires understanding the advocacy argument that each story is trying to make. Many libraries think about addressing deficits—understaffing, too few programs, lack of funding—when creating data stories, but this focus is not the only important goal for a data story. Most library advocacy data stories have one or more of these common goals:

- *Understanding real needs.* This goal is related to what data is already collected and what more might need to be collected or analyzed—including data from other sources, whether local or national—to make possible an understanding of needs based on data as evidence. Evidence of needs might include a lack of resources available in languages spoken in a community, consistent requests from teachers to borrow materials for classroom use, or demographic data that shows low literacy levels in a neighborhood.
- *Serving real needs.* This goal relates to the resources—time, money, further data collection or analysis, and so on—that are necessary to adequately meet measurable needs. Resources might be more books in a language spoken by a large new immigrant group, additional funds to purchase resources for teachers' use, or time to develop a grant proposal for a neighborhood literacy program.

- *Building on strengths.* This is often overlooked as a goal, but it is relevant when, for example, regional investments in industry lead to relationships that make donations for a new children's science exhibit possible. It is also relevant when a library has an unusual collection of rare books, historical archives, or musical instruments to lend to the public.
- *Addressing deficits.* This is a frequent goal that emerges from initial data analysis, such as when a month-by-month comparison of the use of services over several years shows that a previously popular service is declining in use. Both *building on strengths* and *addressing deficits* become possible goals after an assessment of strengths and deficits, and there are many resources to help with this kind of assessment in the library evaluation literature (Fleming-May and Mays 2021; Wright and White 2007; Dresang et al. 2006). Data determines which of these goals are reasonable because any data storytelling goal must align with the reasonable interpretation of data as evidence from a specific context.

Motivations

The second part of the logic of a data story relates to what motivates library staff to tell it. These motivations are about what kinds of messages we expect audiences to understand, remember, and retell. Most library advocacy data stories fall into one of three categories:

1. Sharing achievements
2. Benchmarking
3. Justifying investments

Motivations are our internal answer to the question: What do we hope the story will accomplish for the audience? *Sharing achievements* means demonstrating the impact of funding and other resources, such as showing the increase in funds raised or new relationships started because of adding a new advancement staff position. *Benchmarking* means drawing on comparisons to explain what is needed and why. For example, staff positions in marketing and graphic design have grown over time, motivated by comparisons among midsized and larger libraries, where investments in publicity have helped to sustain or increase library use. *Justification* means to make a compelling case for funding and other resources, like new staff positions. Although there can be additional motivations, these three are useful in that they are very common and logically clear.

Clear goals and motivations also keep the project of the story from becoming too big. When audiences are faced with too much data or wandering storytelling, they tend to zone out, and the work of the story is lost. Identifying and clearly sticking with a particular goal and motivation will give the data story a reasonable scope. Sometimes stories are expected to accomplish more than is feasible for any one form of communication to accomplish; defining a goal and a motivation means grounding the data story in an analytical and logical approach so that the story has the best possible chance of success.

Table 2.2 demonstrates a few of the infinite ways of combining goals and motivations as the fundamentals of effective library data storytelling. Just the process of reflecting on typical goals and motivations—or defining others unique

TABLE 2.2
Data Stories as a Matrix of Motivations and Goals

MOTIVATIONS	GOALS		
	Sharing Achievements	Benchmarking	Justifying Investments
Understanding real needs	Sharing results of a survey showing community literacy needs	Comparing data from peer libraries showing numbers of non-cardholders	Surveying library users to inform priorities for a building expansion
Serving real needs	Sharing results of a successful program that increased community literacy	Launching a library card registration program targeting non-cardholder neighborhoods	Building a larger children's area justified by survey data and comparisons to peer libraries
Building on strengths	Sharing the sustained impact of a longstanding hands-on science exhibit on local science teachers and students	Comparing regional collections and expanding an already strong cookbook collection	Justifying purchase of new play area equipment based on high levels of current use
Addressing deficits	Sharing the six-month impact of a newly established hands-on science exhibit, based on use and teacher feedback	Comparing open hours with peer libraries to discover a need to consider increasing hours of operation	Justifying purchase of books in a language spoken by many community members but underrepresented in collections

to a specific situation—will strengthen the underlying logic of a data story. Goals and motivations are the bones of clear and effective data stories, which are fleshed out by the contexts and arguments that library advocates bring to life for their audience.

Data storytelling approaches are not only important for the stories told outwardly to stakeholders, but they can also inform the process of working with data, from collection through analysis and reporting.

Data Life Cycles, Storytelling Life Cycles

A data life cycle begins from the first thought of data collection, continues through data analysis, flourishes with data storytelling, and concludes in data storage—with potential renaissance through additional data reuse, mining, and sharing. Many librarians are accomplished experts in information storage; some are even global leaders in developing infrastructure for data storage, access, and curation. However, most data experts have not worked extensively with storytelling as a means of informing the deliberate design of a library data life cycle. A full data life cycle means that data is collected, analyzed, communicated in compelling ways, and stored for reuse.

Data Collection with a Storytelling Life Cycle Mindset

Storytelling is a dynamic interactive process of sharing human meaning. It prioritizes interaction over transaction and highlights the value of listening and the potential for a great story to be told repeatedly. Storytelling can extend the life of data, pulling it into a more complete life cycle (see figure 2.1).

A storytelling life cycle is about stories that survive beyond a single telling. Thus, accurate data stories must be rooted in an effective practice of data collection. Data collection in libraries is accomplished in at least three broad ways: automatic, routine, and interactive. Each has different critical implications for seeing power, understanding inequality, and creating greater equity in the data collection process.

Automatic Data Collection

Automatic data collection means data automatically generated by software systems. Generated with minimal human intervention, this data will be consistent

FIGURE 2.1
Data storytelling life cycle

unless the system breaks or is flawed. A classic example is the automatic collection of circulation statistics, which are a key tool in collection development, from evaluation (Adams and Noel 2008) to developing methods of analysis to help manage research collections effectively (Knievel et al. 2006).

Biases inherent in the system of data collection may go unnoticed until there is a problem. For example, digital systems involving cameras rely on technology that has been shown to be biased against people with darker skin colors (Buolamwini and Gebru 2018). Automatic does not necessarily mean neutral, and taking a critical approach to automatic data collection may require some reconsideration of what software and hardware routinely do and how they align with the ethical treatment of people. As automated technologies continue to change, so will laws, policies, and practices.

Routine Data Collection

Routine data collection means data generated by library staff, such as the number of reference questions, which is observed, noted, and recorded in spreadsheets or software. Routine data collection counts are based on making observations, and this kind of data collection takes work, but it does not require making judgments on the fly about what to collect.

For example, library staff routinely count program attendees so they can track trends over time, but they decide in advance if they will, for example, count children and caregivers separately, as when preschool groups come to the library with teachers. On a larger scale, counting the types of programs offered suggests that city libraries are most effective, offering more program types (23.7) than suburban (20 program types) or rural libraries (14 program types), but the "per capita measures tell a more nuanced story. While city libraries offer more annual programs and more types of programs on average, town/rural libraries offer more programs on a per capita basis, making the most of the capacity they have" (Goek 2023). While most routinely collected data is numeric, there can be routinely collected qualitative data as well, such as open-ended satisfaction questionnaires after programs or visits to the library.

Interactive Data Collection

Interactive data collection means systematic collection of data about people's experiences, opinions, preferences, and so on. Interactive data collection processes usually involve more complex forms of data, for example, responses to surveys. In-depth surveys of library user experience, as well as brief one-off requests for information at points of checkout or pop-ups during website use, are all interactive. When library staff informally listen to patrons' experiences and recall those experiences at a staff meeting, those experiences are anecdotes and should not be considered as data. Stories are data when they are collected systematically and with equitable opportunities to participate.

This kind of interaction is easy to forget in a busy library environment. Whose stories are retold depends on who is willing to tell their experience, and that in turn may be influenced by a variety of factors in terms of who is more or less likely to tell library staff about their experience. Systematic opportunities to share experiences, such as open-ended survey questions, represent a good effort to avoid bias in terms of whose stories are heard. Certain kinds of data, like stories about obstacles to using library services, are only available through interactive data collection. Interactions may be minimal, such as a patron writing down their experience on a piece of paper, or they may be detailed and complex, as in the case of conversations, interviews, or focus groups. Interactively collected data is typically qualitative, meaning that it consists of quotations, opinions, experiences, and stories.

For library data storytelling, the process of data collection may be as important as the category of data collected. The step-by-step process of querying an automated system for statistics (*automatic*) supports a data story based on numbers with minimal human intervention. The process of collecting the same data systematically over weeks, months, and years (*routine*) supports a story told by numbers as they relate to library activities such as programs, or (for example) the number of reference questions asked about options for affordable housing. These two kinds of numbers become more meaningful—and easier to recall—when combined with a story about people or families impacted by the social context and the library's services, but these stories can only be powerful if they relate to real people's experiences (*interactive*), whether through open-ended survey questions or through conversations between patrons and staff at the library.

There are many more factors that impact interactive data collection, including critical considerations for data collection through surveys. Before investigating surveys further, it's important to consider what motivates data collection processes in libraries.

Common Library Data Collection Needs

Whether the audience is a mayor, a board of trustees, a college president, a city council, or an ad hoc committee, library data needs storytelling. Data stories are often told in real time with immediate consequences for how boards vote (for or against) on support for funding, staff, and programs. Data collection can support advocacy, but that depends on what the data is and how it is interpreted. Examples of library data collection needs are shown in table 2.3. Libraries commonly collect data (or explore data collected by library-related organizations; see table 2.4 in the next section) to justify their funding requests.

Data analysis can make patterns clear and visible that are otherwise obscured by the everyday experience of life in an information organization. There are many tools for and approaches to data analysis. Some libraries can afford sophisticated tools that require ongoing subscriptions (e.g., Qualtrics, Tableau, or Power BI), while others may take advantage of free data visualization tools and toolkits (e.g., Google's Looker Data Studio). Most library staff conducting data analysis

TABLE 2.3
Common Library Data Collection Needs

CATEGORIES	COMMON DATA COLLECTED
Budgets	• For staff • For technology and services • For marketing and PR
Community engagement and outreach	• Programs offered • Services offered • Partnerships between organizations
Foundations	• Donations • Endowments • Other fund sources that augment base funding
Physical plant	• Building improvements • Hours of service • Hours of greatest/least use
Use of library services	• Circulation • Computer use • Program attendance • Cardholders (and non-cardholders)

will use spreadsheets and Excel at early stages in their analytic processes. While this chapter focuses on those for data storytelling, detailed guidance for library data analysis is available in the Further Readings list at the end of this chapter.

Library Data at Different Scales

Library data stories benefit from looking at data from beyond an individual library, benchmarking against similar institutions. Arguments about what improvements should be made need data specific to a particular library, but those arguments are usually more powerful when combined with national- or state-level library data, or data about the social context of a particular library. There are many kinds of library data. Some types of data about libraries have been consistently collected for years by dedicated nonprofit library professional organizations. Data collection at a large scale can help individuals and groups

TABLE 2.4
Library Organizations and Publicly Available Data

LIBRARY ORGANIZATIONS	DATA AND TOOLS AVAILABLE
Institute of Museum and Library Services (IMLS)	• Library Search & Compare • Public Library Survey (PLS) • State Library Administrative Agency (SLAA) Survey
Public Library Association (PLA)	• Project Outcome (free toolkit for sharing library impact) • PLA Benchmark (every public library has an account with free basic access, and an additional subscription option provides custom data visualizations)
Association of College and Research Libraries (ACRL)	• Academic Library Trends and Statistics Survey • ACRL Benchmark (every college and research library has an account with free basic access, and an additional subscription option provides custom data visualizations)
Other	• State libraries • State-level professional library organizations • Regional consortia, systems, or networks

who need evidence of libraries' impact at national and state, regional, and local levels.

National and State Data

Data from large-scale projects can provide a rich picture of the present and history of libraries, individually, comparatively, and on average. Each of the organizations shown in table 2.4 has invested years of time in building an infrastructure for library data and offers valuable services, many of them free and publicly available—although subscription options like Benchmark offer an impressive array of functions for data visualization at an affordable annual cost for most public and academic libraries.

These large-scale library data projects range from data sources (e.g., the Public Library Survey), to fully developed guides for collecting, analyzing, and using data to measure the benefits that libraries provide to their communities (e.g., Project Outcome), to quick and easy tools for comparison (e.g., PLA Benchmark and ACRL Benchmark). As newer tools for comparison, PLA and ACRL Benchmark also include trend comparisons to national averages and to an automatically selected set of peer libraries. These last two tools require subscriptions to utilize their full potential, because the power of these tools requires significant ongoing development work. However, Benchmark has a limited set of tools available to all libraries for free.

The downside to these incredible data sources is the sense of being over-whelmed that they can generate because of their richness and scale. It can be difficult to know where to start, especially for those who are less familiar with large-scale data sets. And for people who are data experts, it can be difficult to know where to stop! For all audiences, presenting large numbers without enough context or meaning can lead to disengagement with data, which is one reason why understanding and using stories and storytelling are so necessary for libraries.

Regional Data

One level down in scale is regional data, which usually means a set of towns, cities, or counties that share a geographic area. This is at a higher level than local data because, for example, there will be multiple libraries, school districts, or municipalities collecting data that is similar but not overlapping. Regional data is helpful when looking for comparisons with neighboring governments or institutions. Library funding is frequently generated, sustained, allocated, or at least supplemented by donations from people who have fond memories of the library and still live in the region. Even academic libraries at research institutions whose graduates are highly geographically dispersed will still find some donors with strong regional ties, through family connections. Data resources at the regional level can help to identify community demographics for public libraries, locate potential funders, and support arguments for how libraries act as part of the regional infrastructure. Sources for regional data include:

- school districts
- Head Start preschools
- crisis nurseries

- park districts
- transit systems
- food banks and pantries
- housing services
- nursing homes

Data collected by regional community groups, organizations, or institutions can provide a richer picture of how libraries matter to their communities as well as who is not yet connected to libraries and could be. Each type of data will have some value for library planning. For example, preschool and school district data is valuable for considering the population of children and families who need early childhood literacy programming at the library. Data from transit systems will help in understanding patterns of library building use, including barriers to access. This list does not include every regionally significant data source. For example, another source might be regional studies of internet use by reputable research groups like the Pew Foundation (Pew Research Center 2003).

Regional data can demonstrate how a particular library or system of libraries relates to its immediate neighboring geographic context. Most regional data analysis is a matter of thinking about the infrastructures of the community. An environmental scan of a community will examine how the library fits into the larger contexts, from internet access to housing and use of public resources. For example, in a community with an aging population, the data may support arguments for stronger bookmobile or home-delivery services. Even when extreme budget cuts have diminished publicly funded systems of support, looking for support functions wherever they exist will help to situate what the library offers as part of a larger community ecosystem. These data may also reveal opportunities for collaboration between the library and other organizations (McDowell 2019).

Inevitably, regional data will have been collected in a variety of ways, and so the library's goal is to use it to see trends and patterns rather than expecting to see precise agreements across various data sets. Regional data is complex, and it can be difficult to untangle all the overlapping contextual elements, even in a relatively small region. For example, social geographic issues, such as the ongoing legacy of historical redlining practices that continue to affect racial distribution in housing, provide an underlying context for neighborhood diversity and even past decisions about library location. Even more, for example, the unpredictable COVID-19 pandemic in 2020–22 led to sudden unemployment spikes, which overwhelmed library resources and made it seem impossible to use data for planning. In the long run, however, regional data is a powerful way to plan for library impact and demonstrate responsiveness to regional needs.

Local Data

Local data is from the institution itself or from related organizations in the same community that collect data overlapping with the population that the institution serves. Local data is valuable for storytelling because it is meaningful to people, not only as descriptors of their own community, but also as a way of staying in dialogue with other members of the community. For example, local data about community broadband costs, access, and usage can help to inform library investments, especially when there are known needs coming from households that lack access or face high costs for access. In some communities, broadband access is initially cheaper if subscribers rent rather than buy equipment, but this setup can leave the poorest subscribers with ongoing rental costs that ultimately make their internet access more expensive. Some donors are motivated by the idea that their dollars can make a direct, local impact, with the evidence of local data demonstrating needs.

Local data collected interactively, like experiences of past cultural programs or input about future program plans, can be shared as part of the story of and publicity for events. Interactive local data comes from people in a community, and the stories they tell can go immediately back to that built-in audience. People complete library surveys because they care or have something pressing to share, and those people are the first and best audience for data storytelling about the results. When done with audiences in mind, data collection provides an opportunity to connect and share what was learned with people who are already invested in knowing more. This data often avoids the trap of numbing audiences with large numbers by zooming in on the people and questions that matter most to those in a particular place.

At the same time, library impact stories will always involve audiences of those who control resources, as democratic representatives or through systems of power (and responsibility) with long histories. Library workers whose positions are lower in the hierarchy, as well as those in middle management, face special challenges in collecting data. They may be tasked with data collection without having much input into how the process should happen or what data might best serve the library's needs. They may also have collected significant amounts of data already, but different groups may disagree about whether that is the right data or how it is interpreted.

Within a library, there can be vastly different understandings of the value of data and its interpretation. For example, one librarian shared a story of having presented data to leadership that was intended to support hiring an additional staff position. When the leaders reviewed the data, they instead argued to cut one of the existing staff positions and hire part-time staff. Data storytelling can be a process of working through such disparate interpretations so that the intended outcomes are narrated with the data. When stakeholders—including those tasked with collecting data—are invited to explain their interpretations and listen to each other's stories, it is possible to have a shared storytelling process so that a collaboratively generated story of what the data means for the future of the library can emerge.

When using data collected from people, or when taking data from people yourselves, it is good ethical practice to give back to the people who participate. When collecting survey data, it is also a best practice to be aware of the time sacrifice you're asking from diverse community members who might already face discrimination. Strive to find mutually beneficial ways to invite diverse survey participants, while remembering that social biases are attitudes with real systemic consequences. Many people in the United States today have little free time because they are living in poverty despite working multiple jobs, or are working full-time despite profound health challenges that require as much rest as possible to prepare and recuperate for the next day of work. Seek ways to connect with diverse communities while being mindful and respectful that biases accumulate, especially for people and families who face multiple forms of discrimination at once. Always invite people to participate in a survey, but try not to presume or demand it (see box 2.1).

BOX 2.1

Tips for Thoughtfully Representing People as Data

The same critical approaches that apply to the thoughtful representation of people as human beings should apply to data storytelling. Data represents people just as much as movies, advertisements, children's books, and any other form of media do. Many characteristics of people in each library community are profoundly important to providing good service, so it is reasonable that libraries would represent them as data.

(continued on p. 40)

Box 2.1 (continued)

- *Who you are as storyteller matters.* Speaking about a group that includes oneself is very different than speaking about a group that does not. Sharing some elements of one's identity but not others—such as geography, race, class—should be acknowledged transparently and humbly. Having personal experience as a member of a group can be helpful to telling a story, but that does not give the storyteller license to speak for or characterize others.
- *Do your homework.* Be aware of biases and stereotypes that people face every day. Not considering race will lead to data representation that reproduces culturally familiar biases about people. If you are not subject to these biases, you will need to do extra homework to understand what they are, how they are harmful, and how to humanize all audience members.
- *Listening is key, but demanding or expecting that others explain to you the biases related to their identity is unfair.* Speak respectfully, and listen when corrected, but do not direct others to explain to you why or how your representation is biased. If you are unaware of injustices based on a specific kind of identity, then take time to learn about them.
- *Excellent data about people is nuanced, just like excellent representations.* Look for opportunities to be nuanced, specific, and humanizing in your representations.
- *Always question data analyses that blame groups of people.* Avoid aligning data stories with stereotypes implying that the social conditions that negatively affect people are their fault. Be wary of blame in data storytelling generally, as it carries bias and ultimately undermines the credibility of the analysis.
- *When in doubt, be humble.* Representation is hard work, and it's wise to be humble and keep improving. Representation is important, and it is one valuable way that library data can contribute to conversations that look critically at causes of social problems, processes, and conditions.

Surveys as Critical Interactive Data Collection

Surveys are one of the most common forms of data collection. Libraries regularly generate their own data through patron and community surveys.

Surveys should involve interaction, not just extraction. Ethical data collection requires critical insights to ensure that it is equitable. Collection processes often rely on unexamined assumptions about what is worth counting and what can be counted. Design of data collection instruments and processes should include consideration of the ways that counting is the result of a set of decisions. What "counts" is always socially constructed (Stone 2020). Data is comprised of facts, and what counts as a fact is itself historically constructed (Poovey 1998).

Sometimes the understanding of data as facts becomes skewed in ways that amplify threats and under-emphasize positive elements (Rosling et al. 2018). Other times, data can obscure or even hide threats that pose extreme danger to some groups in communities because they are not the dominant groups. Audiences in this process help pilot surveys, and diverse audiences who provide honest feedback about the data collection process are important. They can provide insight into how the process may represent or erase their interests. Diverse perspectives can transform a survey from a routine process to a way of connecting with people accurately and authentically, as an organization.

Here we are not talking about formal survey research, but about local library surveys. Local surveys are designed to answer questions about the library and its connection to the community it serves. This kind of dialogue can thrive in many forms, whether in a formal question-and-answer session after a presentation or, to borrow from "passive programming," on a bulletin board with sticky notes for patrons to leave their thoughts about recent library changes. Connecting library changes to patron input not only justifies those changes, but it also demonstrates that the library is invested in ongoing communication with the community.

Good storytelling ethics include respect for the source of the story. Sometimes people tell their own personal stories about the library and how it is important to them. When this storytelling happens spontaneously, it is good to be prepared with (1) a positive response and appreciation for sharing, and (2) a request to retell a really good story (often anonymously) to help other people learn how beneficial the library can be. This encouragement to keep telling does not have to be complicated; it can be as simple as saying, "What an amazing story! Would you mind if I shared it with our library director?" If they agree, then ask: "Would you like me to give you credit or should I share it anonymously?" If they want credit, be sure to ask for the name they would like you to use and contact information so that you can stay in touch. Most people will agree to share their stories anonymously. See box 2.2 for information on how people's stories can be data.

Data Storytelling Survey Steps

No matter what the range or types of data collected, incorporating data storytelling practices will yield better relationships with the community. Incorporating data storytelling into a normal survey process changes the work necessary for a successful survey process. Specifically, data storytelling focused on survey work will sustain engagement with the audience surveyed as the audience for the resulting data stories. This work requires a six-step process:

1. Develop the survey from initial idea to pilot survey for revisions.
2. Finalize the survey, launch it, and publicize it widely.
3. Sustain ongoing publicity up to the end of data collection.
4. Collect, analyze, and report results, offering respondents an opportunity to sign up to receive results when they complete the survey.
5. Construct the results as one or more data stories about how the results were used and what changed.
6. Ask the audience for further feedback on those changes.

These general steps are a reasonable guide, but they may be modified depending on many factors, including the size of the community. Stories travel differently at different scales, and data storytelling strategies must similarly be adapted to the scale of the participants and audience.

Community Size and Survey Strategies

When a data collection process incorporates storytelling principles and considers audiences as fundamental to survey design, then the scale of the process matters. Large- and medium-sized communities' libraries have different audiences from small libraries. Large and medium libraries can distribute longer surveys effectively, as audiences will implicitly understand that the library needs data at a certain scale to be able to inform its decision-making. These libraries—public

BOX 2.2
Are People's Stories Data?

We know that stories can be constructed from data, and story structures are key to effectively communicating the interpretation of data. Let's imagine that an open-ended survey question is designed to collect stories about people whose lives were transformed because of the library. A story like this may provide a powerful illustration of how the library matters to the community. Stories as survey responses force us to ask: Is a person's individual story really data? Here are some key elements of contrast between a person's story and the library's data.

Person's Story	Library's Data
Belongs to the person	Belongs to the organization
Is told in a specific context of communication	Is collected to travel across communication contexts
Is specific to the lived experience of an individual person	Is gathered to identify patterns and trends that lead to insights

Even in a survey response, a person's story should not be treated in the same way that numeric/quantitative or even anonymized qualitative data is treated. When collecting rich qualitative data that might include a person's story, the best practice is to offer some way for the person to indicate whether they agree to or decline the possible reuse of their story for library promotion purposes. This section of the survey could include a checkbox where people can indicate that their story may be retold (or not) anonymously, or include the option to collect contact information to give credit. More on these concepts appears in chapter 4 in the discussion of whose story it is to tell.

and academic—can benefit from previously designed surveys available through Project Outcome, which are available for copying by creating a free sign-in at projectoutcome.org.

In a very small and interconnected community, however, distributing a survey with pages of questions could seem impersonal or cold. Instead, consider asking the community for input through questions (on paper or with a simple form on a tablet) at checkout, by visiting community groups in person, or by setting up a table anyplace people are already gathering—at the farmer's market, baseball or football fields, festivals, and so on. In all cases, the results should be communicated back to the community for their ongoing input to create the best potential for a dialogue between library and community.

In library data collection, one of the key ways to keep a dialogue between library and community alive is to be mindful of the obstacles to dialogue, which can occur when collecting data from people and receiving input.

Survey Fatigue and Input Fatigue

Some businesses, such as health care, car repair, and other service-focused industries, have forced brief surveys into every interaction, whether online or via phone. Practices like these can lead to *survey fatigue,* in which audiences stop responding because they have become overwhelmed by or numb to requests for input. On the other hand, libraries have a wide array of responsibilities that may lead to *input fatigue,* the experience of being overwhelmed by community input to a point of exhaustion that precludes good listening and data analysis. One of the best ways to combat both survey fatigue and input fatigue is to keep surveys short and focused, calculating the time needed to read and analyze open-ended responses to the survey. For survey participation and completion, shorter is almost always better.

Library surveys should strive to be engaging and inviting to their communities, while avoiding constantly requesting input to avoid survey fatigue. Although libraries can't control the environment of survey practices that impact communities, they can be judicious in considering that environment when discerning when and how often to survey their communities. For example, the weeks around major school holidays can be distracting transition times for parents. It is good practice to have some trusted allies in the community who receive (and frequently complete) library surveys and who can offer input into the timing of surveys across a range of demographic groups.

Libraries with a long history of community surveys will be familiar with input fatigue. Some people will take advantage of an invitation to give input and flood a staff member (or an open-ended written question) with their frustrations and anxieties, whether related to the library or not. Remember that a survey is a kind of contract for a limited, specific interaction. Conversational approaches to input, either digital or on paper, do not mean an agreement to fully address every possible verbal (or written) complaint; they are simply a way of listening.

The goal of a survey is to gather data, so some patrons may need a reminder that, unless they complete the survey, staff won't be able to include their input. In an in-person interaction that induces input fatigue, staff should have the freedom to say, gently but firmly: "This is such specific and detailed input! I don't want to miss your intention, so would you consider writing that down on this form?" or "Would you consider completing our additional customer feedback survey?" Similarly, open-ended responses that are irrelevant or only loosely connected to the topic of the survey may be discarded. If possible, it is good practice to have two people read open-ended responses to determine what can be analyzed or discarded.

Conclusion: Data Life Cycles and Healthy Internal Library Conversations

In a spring 2023 workshop with colleagues from multiple libraries, a woman described the difficulty she had in getting data from the expert who collected and analyzed it at her library. She asked for advice on how to persuade her colleague to share the data. Immediately, another hand in the room shot up. The second person introduced themself as the data expert at another library, and their frustration was that nobody ever asked for the data, or when they did, they wanted a simple numeric answer taken out of context. We discussed the importance of acknowledging the depth of work behind any well-crafted data interpretation, and several insights emerged.

First, people often imagine that a specific data point will be a decisive factor, so they request very specific data without knowing the context needed for accurate interpretation. Second, people approach reports based on data as the launching point for a broader discussion, and ultimately they request more data collection before they have fully absorbed the meaning of the previous data.

Data experts steward data, but they also have important context: *knowledge*. We came to a shared understanding of the frustration of data experts in libraries that looks something like this: Colleagues who are intimidated by data try to steer the conversation to something more familiar or speculate about what other data could be gathered. A data expert, understandably frustrated by this dynamic, might become reluctant to share data with those with less expertise, leading to communication disconnects that become a structural problem for a library.

With that compassionate framing, the conversation really began to take off, and people in the workshop began to discuss how they could fully engage with a library data expert's work. We came to agree that when an expert presents data along with what story the data tells—the analysis, collection process, and other work that creates a rigorous data life cycle—it is vital for colleagues to respect that work.

FURTHER READINGS

Kellam, Lynda M., and Kristi Thompson, eds. 2016. *Databrarianship: The Academic Data Librarian in Theory and Practice*. American Library Association. www.alastore.ala.org/content/databrarianship-academic-data-librarian-theory-and-practice.

    Covers the data life cycle from collection development to preservation, examines the challenges of working with different forms of data, and explores service models suited to a variety of library types.

Magnuson, Lauren, ed. 2016. *Data Visualization: A Guide to Visual Storytelling for Libraries*. Rowman & Littlefield. https://rowman.com/ISBN/9781442271104/Data-Visualization-A-Guide-to-Visual-Storytelling-for-Libraries.

    A practical guide to the skills and tools needed to create beautiful and meaningful visual stories through data visualization.

Rice, Robin, and John Southall. 2016. *The Data Librarian's Handbook*. Facet. www.alastore.ala.org/content/data-librarians-handbook.

    Offers practical guidance on how to collect, curate, and crunch data for economic, social, and scientific purposes.

REFERENCES

Adams, Brian, and Bob Noel. 2008. "Circulation Statistics in the Evaluation of Collection Development." *Collection Building* 27, no. 2: 71–73. https://doi.org/10.1108/01604950810870227.

Buolamwini, Joy, and Timnit Gebru. 2018. "Gender Shades: Intersectional Accuracy Disparities in Commercial Gender Classification." *Proceedings of the 1st Conference on Fairness, Accountability and Transparency, Proceedings of Machine Learning Research* 81: 77–91. https://proceedings.mlr.press/v81/buolamwini18a.html.

Dresang, Eliza T., Melissa Gross, and Leslie Edmonds Holt. 2006. *Dynamic Youth Services Through Outcome-Based Planning and Evaluation*. American Library Association.

Emory Libraries. 2023. "You Spoke, We Listened: Libraries Respond to User Survey Results with Improvements." Emory News Center December 4. https://news.emory.edu/stories/2023/12/er_library_improvements_04-12-2023/story.html.

Fleming-May, Rachel A., and Regina Mays. 2021. *Fundamentals of Planning and Assessment for Libraries*. American Library Association.

Goek, Sara S. 2023. "Public Library Services for Strong Communities Report: Results from the 2022 PLA Annual Survey." Public Library Association. www.ala.org/pla/sites/ala.org.pla/files/content/data/PLA_Services_Survey_Report_2023.pdf.

Knievel, Jennifer E., Heather Wicht, and Lynn Silipigni Connaway. 2006. "Use of Circulation Statistics and Interlibrary Loan Data in Collection Management." *College & Research Libraries* 67, no. 1: 35–49. https://doi.org/10.5860/crl.67.1.35.

McDowell, Kate. 2019. "Teaching 'between': Reflections on Learning Inter-Organizational Collaboration." *Education for Information* 25, no. 2: 149–53. https://doi.org/10.3233/EFI-180239.

McDowell, Kate, Xinhui Hu, and Matthew J. Turk. 2024. "Developing Library and Data Storytelling Toolkits: Scenarios and Personas." *Wisdom, Well-Being, Win-Win – 19th International Conference, iConference 2024, Proceedings*. Springer.

National Storytelling Network. n.d. "Hire a Storyteller." https://storynet.org/find-a-storyteller/.

Pew Research Center. 2003. "Internet Use by Region in the U.S." www.pewresearch.org/internet/2003/08/27/internet-use-by-region-in-the-u-s/.

Poovey, Mary. 1998. *History of the Modern Fact: Problems of Knowledge in the Sciences of Wealth and Society*. University of Chicago Press.

Rosling, Hans, with Ola Rosling and Anna Rosling Rönnlund. 2018. *Factfulness: Ten Reasons We're Wrong about the World—and Why Things Are Better Than You Think*. Flatiron Books.

Stone, Deborah. 2020. *Counting: How We Use Numbers to Decide What Matters*. Liverite.

Wright, S., and L. S. White. 2007. *SPEC Kit 303: Library Assessment*. Association of Research Libraries.

NOTE

1. This chapter draws from and expands upon research conducted as part of an Institute of Museum and Library Services planning grant, finding ways to make data storytelling work for practicing librarians. The initial launch workshop had 680 participants, most of them from the United States and Canada, with a few people joining from the Philippines, the United Kingdom, and Australia. The forty-member Core Design Team (CDT) worked with the research team over a series of workshops from fall 2022 to fall 2024.

3

Narrative Strategies
Classic Structures, Plots, and Revision Process

n fall 2016, I gave a presentation on data storytelling to early-career engineering professors. Engineers deal with rich and complex data that has real-world implications for creating safe buildings, bridges, planes, and more. They solve problems by finding the correct answers, or at least a correct range of answers, that will ensure that the materials work.

In my presentation, I explained that the same data story can, accurately and honestly, be told in different ways. And in fact, the audience will be more likely to trust the storyteller if they are able to tell a story flexibly, using the same data with different emphases in response to their audience. One hand shot up in the audience, and the professor asked: "You mean people will trust you more if you tell the story different ways?" "That's right!" I replied. If the information in the story remains the same, then being able to tell the story in different ways will build your audience's trust in your understanding of what you are communicating.

For example, an effective advocacy story about increasing funding for a library program that benefits people with physical mobility issues could be presented as a one-paragraph budget request with the necessary funding numbers. Or it could be told as a presentation that provides demographic data about people with physical disabilities in the service district of the library and a visual map of the physical paths that a person using a walker, wheelchair, or cane or needing door-opening assistance must take to enter/exit the library for a program. It could also be told as a story of a person—real or hypothetical, named with enthusiastic consent or completely anonymized—whose life changed when a library renovation replaced old, crowded shelves with spacious aisles. If anonymized, an illustration could include maps of the differences, showing the routes by which a child who uses a wheelchair could access every book in the building. There are many ways to tell the same story, and being able to tell that story in different ways, especially in response to live questions at presentations, will build trust between teller and audience.

Story both is and is not a technical solution to a communication problem. On the one hand, stories are felt as a whole narrative experience that is difficult to break down into components. They carry informational and emotional content at the same time, creating a much richer experience for audiences than dry data presentation alone. In this sense, we know stories when we see them. On the other hand, stories are technical, built from patterns (including characters, settings, and plots), and organized in recognizable and often classic narrative structures. Knowing these patterns and understanding how they work to convey information effectively—that is, knowing the range of structures that will carry the material of the story—requires some technical understanding of narrative.

This chapter is about the materials of story-building that can create a great narrative experience out of data. Because there are many different ways that our minds grasp data and narrative, it is important to explore multiple ways of thinking about story-building. In my fifteen years of experience teaching story-telling, I've consistently encountered three ways of thinking among information professionals: story-focused, data-focused, and iterative revision from data to story. We will walk through these ways of thinking and explore the ways that narratives can be built by (1) borrowing classic narrative structures, (2) focusing on data and plot development, and (3) using a process of iterative revision. These ways can be combined; for example, an iterative revision process can improve a narrative built from classic structures.

The following sections briefly introduce these three ways as broad strategies for building data stories. First, we will learn classic narrative structures—transformation, continuity, and discovery—and their interactions with information and emotion—starting from concrete examples of donor stories. Then we will explore building stories by focusing on the middle of the story—where the narrative often gets lost. After that, we will examine the iterative revision process and look at the Storytelling-Data-Information-Knowledge-Wisdom (S-DIKW) framework as a way to build a strong foundation for a data story. Finally, we will contend with the reality that stories are not neutral, and we will introduce counter-storytelling concepts and strategies for creating greater social justice.

Before delving deeper into each of the three narrative strategies in turn, we must consider the audience. Together, informational and emotional elements constitute the audience's experience of a story. The process of developing a story is not the same, chronologically, as the process of an audience experiencing a story, so it is valuable to begin from an understanding of audience experience.

Information and Emotion in Storytelling

In good data storytelling, the story increases in both information and emotion over the time of its delivery. In other words, the chronological delivery of information is constantly paired with increased emotional content. This is the most basic principle of storytelling: Both information and emotion should contribute to the momentum of a story, from the beginning through to the climax and finally the resolution.

The visual depiction of a story arc in figure 3.1 implies the movement of time, or story chronology, from left to right. The story arc is shaped with a line that moves upward from left to right, to indicate that the audience receives more information and experiences greater emotional engagement over time. After the peak moment of information and emotion, at the end of the story, both elements decrease slightly, offering the audience a moment to experience the resolution. However a story is developed, the audience should have this experience of interwoven information and emotion over time. This ensures that audiences can retell the stories they hear and become library advocacy storytellers themselves.

In a world of ever more complex data, there is no one universal narrative or way of thinking about narrative that fits every situation. Any of the strategies presented in this chapter will interweave information with emotion. They can be combined in one story development process when teams consisting of different kinds of thinkers work together. We will start with the first strategy, classic narrative structures, and consider how each structure connects to concrete examples of donor stories.

Three Classic Narrative Structures

Classic structures, the first of the three strategies by which narratives can be built, cover three time-honored and effective *narrative structures* that provide adaptable templates for organizing the informational and emotional content of

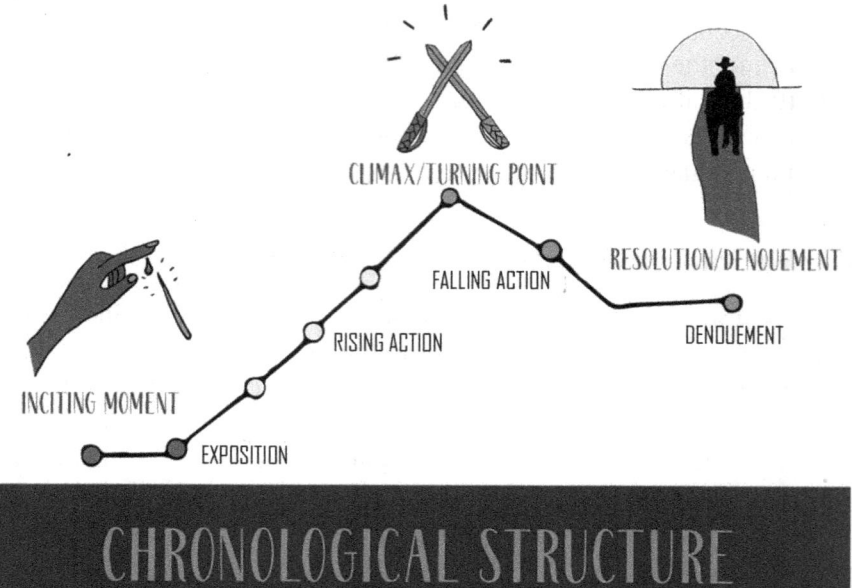

FIGURE 3.1
Increased information and emotion

Source: Hilary Pope

library data stories. The three types of narrative structure are those of *transformation*, *continuity*, and *discovery*. Transformation stories are about change and the feeling of awe when people reach heroic achievements. Continuity stories are about how institutions last, sustaining their services through turbulent times. Discovery stories are about engaging the audience with a mystery and the satisfaction of discovering new information. Through my eight years of workshops and six years of teaching data storytelling, these three narrative structures have proven to be succinct yet meaningful ways to leverage existing understandings of narrative, or classic narrative structures, as shown in table 3.1.

Making use of these ideas does not require, for example, all seventeen steps in the hero's journey from Joseph Campbell's narrative analysis of the legendary life stories of major religious figures around the world (Campbell 1949). We need to extend cultural humility and avoid universalizing in ways that overwrite perspectives with singular narratives (Adichie 2009). Cultural

TABLE 3.1
Describing Narrative Structures

NARRATIVE STRUCTURE	ORIGINATING THEORY	EMOTIONAL IMPACT
Transformation	Joseph Campbell's *The Hero with a Thousand Faces*	Awe at transformation, joy of watching a hero triumph
Continuity	Tzvetan Todorov's *The Fantastic*	Reassurance, stability, and resilience despite challenges
Discovery	Roland Barthes's *S/Z*	Mystery, suspense, intrigue, and satisfaction of coming to understanding

humility in structuring narratives means acknowledging our own limitations as storytellers. We will not know or be able to represent all the cultural ways of knowing. Instead, the approach here draws from definitions of cultural humility as based on "deep listening and reflection without defensiveness" (Hurley et al. 2022, 29). The three ways of describing narratives discussed here are neither universal nor complete. They can describe a vast array of stories, but they do not describe all stories. They draw from major theorists in narratology, literary criticism, folklore, and semiotics, and they can support the crafting of an effective data story by demonstrating ways to interweave a story's informational content with its emotional tone.

The Transformation Story

Transformation stories are triumphant, told after the fact of a major transition and in celebration of what was accomplished. A common example is that of a successful fundraising campaign. There are many data stories embedded in any fundraising campaign, including how many people donated overall, how many people donated at different levels of contribution, and how a few major gifts enabled the library to move from speculative dreams to real changes in infrastructure. The beginning of this story structure emphasizes trouble and obstacles, as shown in figure 3.2. The middle provides a sense of action, and often struggle, to overcome challenges. The ending is one of successful accomplishment, with a feeling of awe.

A typical transformation story is the hero's journey. A hero encounters obstacles and is transformed in the process of overcoming them (Campbell 1949). The emotional impact of a hero's journey story is the joy of watching someone do the impossible, which might include sustaining a seemingly impossible level of dedication to service over many years. In superhero stories, from Wonder Woman to Spider-Man, there is joy in seeing the impossible made possible through their supernatural powers. This narrative structure is appropriate in any data story that involves awe at transformation, wonder at scale, or marvelous accomplishments.

Libraries, however, do not always make great heroes to outside audiences. Although libraries transform, and those who transform them see their work as

FIGURE 3.2
The transformation story

Source: Xinhui Hu

heroic, the library itself doesn't always translate well as a hero to others. Why? Because the way this story structure works typically involves a person who transforms by triumphing over obstacles. The library is more like a helper character, the mysterious figure who appears on the path just in time, provides the magical key to unlock barriers ahead, and then disappears again into the background. The library is the helper in stories of success. The people are the heroes.

For example, at a storytelling workshop, a librarian shared the story of two parents of young children, both of whom were working full-time and earning degrees at a community college. They found the library to be an important resource and refuge. Despite having intense class and work schedules, this family came to the library regularly, and the library's policy supported the couple's bringing their children with them to the study areas. Over time, the parents triumphed, and both parents earned their degrees (see box 3.1). The library was the helper to their heroic feats.

BOX 3.1
Lifelong Learners, Lifelong Earners

Statistically, people who complete any degree after high school tend to have higher lifelong earnings. A bachelor's degree leads, on average, to lifetime earnings that are 84 percent higher than those with a high school diploma. College graduation also benefits society as a whole. People with bachelor's degrees are 24 percent more likely to be employed and three-and-a-half times less likely to live in poverty. Even more striking, a college graduate will, on average, contribute $381,000 more in taxes than they receive in benefits over the course of their lifetime (Association of Public & Land-Grant Universities, n.d.). Any time a library helps a person or family complete a college degree, it is contributing not just to lifelong learning but also to lifelong *earning*. More libraries should proclaim the ways that their open-door and safe study spaces contribute to the well-being of communities financially.

Donor Funding as a Transformation Story

A transformation narrative can blend information and emotion in library story-telling by, for example, telling the story of a donor-funded new library building. There are several ways to sustain emotional engagement here. The first is to start with the struggle of the old building's decay. The beginning details the old building's specific problems: a leaky room, an outdated HVAC system, and shelving that precludes wheelchair access. This part is followed by the struggle of communicating the importance of fixing the building to potential donors (which continues until a solution or donor is found). This usually involves some back-and-forth as different attempts are made to engage donors. Then a catalyst—a group of volunteer fundraisers, a wealthy donor, a successful vote on a tax increase, or any combination of catalysts—emerges and provides the necessary funds. The end of the story is triumph at the transformation of the library from the old building to the new building. This story can be told as a celebration of what can be done when people come together to make change, narrating a transformation of the whole community through the heroic work of donors.

Emotions of the Transformation Structure

Most of the time, transformation stories are feel-good tales of how the library helped a person realize their dreams. But transformation stories can also be awful instead of awe-inspiring. For example, the worsening white supremacy movements associated with attacking or even criminalizing intellectual free-dom in the United States are horrific stories of social transformation that will have long-lasting consequences for society if not addressed through policy and legislation.

Libraries have weathered such attacks in the past, as when McCarthy-era censorship instigated an era of quiet resistance among youth services librarians (Jenkins 1995). While the attacks of the present require more active resistance, the ways that libraries have contributed to sustaining an ethos of intellectual freedom historically remain important. Stories of individual librarians who have spent their lives in public service make excellent heroes, but through a different kind of narrative: the continuity story.

The Continuity Story

Imagine a library that survives a hurricane. When the story starts, the library is in a steady state, and all is well. Then a hurricane hits and everything becomes chaotic, with power outages, flooding, and road damage. Gradually, library staff assess the damage to the library building and systems. They check on staff and their community infrastructure. Then they plan and execute steps toward recovery. In the end, the library makes it back to a steady state again, so that equilibrium is restored. This is a classic continuity story, with the emotional satisfaction of confidence in an institution that lasts.

The equilibrium concept comes from narrative theory about the structure of the fantastic (Todorov and Weinstein 1969). The concept of continuity in this book is informed by many retellings of a story called "The Stonecutter," in which a person makes a series of wishes to have more power and becomes many things—a prince, the sun, a cloud, a mountain—only to ultimately return full circle to work as a stonecutter (Sturm 2008).[1] The emotional message of the equilibrium structure is resilience or stability despite challenges. This structure is often used when narrating an institution's history—from its founding through struggle to the present day—or a family's history, or even species survival despite seasons of famine, plague, and disaster. Figure 3.3 shows how a continuity story also works as a story of disaster recovery.

FIGURE 3.3
The continuity story

Source: Xinhui Hu

A continuity story can have a hero, such as Bernice Davis Fiske. She was the children's librarian from 1927 to 1972 at the Urbana Free Library in Urbana, Illinois, the first public library where I worked. I met parents who had grown up with Fiske and were bringing their children back to the same library. Since her retirement, a plaque on the wall celebrates and honors her long, continuous career, which created a sense of welcome and stability for generations of children. Even after a major renovation years after Fiske had passed away, the plaque was reinstalled. Some of the most important heroes in the histories of institutions are those quiet, legendary people who persevere despite incredible changes in society, technology, and world history.

The typical continuity story structure is a cycle. These stories are journeys first from stability to disruption and then forward to a new stability or equilibrium. Think of the worldwide events between 1927 and 1972, including two world wars, the Great Depression, and the Cold War. Children's librarianship has always changed with the times, but a continuity story emphasizes what persists despite disruption. From wars to natural disasters, libraries persist, consistently recovering to serve again.

The typical feeling of this narrative structure is the assurance of long continuity, but this structure also works for troubling stories about the persistence of injustice. For example, in many places, the overlap of poverty and geography continues, generation after generation, and extreme economic inequities mean that some people hardly own anything at all. People who need the public library and everything it provides the most can't always access it. Neighborhoods where good people work multiple jobs to help their families thrive as best as they can are often those that also lack adequate and affordable public transportation. Children from every neighborhood should easily be able to get to the library and back home again safely, so this story structure leads to an argument about what should be done.

In the work of libraries, consider the repeated stories of how burnout overwhelmingly affects BIPOC colleagues (Cooke 2014; Cooke 2019), with no systemic amelioration in sight. Listeners should also experience a negative sense of awe at the scope and scale of racism's presence in library employment trends over time. The call to action in negative continuity stories like these depends on transformation or discovery, and these narratives can be interwoven.

Donor Funding as a Continuity Story

Another donor funding story might emphasize continuing the life of a long-lasting building. This approach is particularly appropriate when funding exists for building renovations, but the building itself is designated for historical preservation. For example, a retired librarian told me a story about a library building renovation plan that involved a debate over how many seats should be provided for patrons. Although the community's population had grown the building had not, leading to overcrowding and, at busy times, no place to sit. She looked back in the historical archives and discovered the ratio of students to seats in the library over fifty years ago. She proposed that the addition to the building use as its key metric the ratio of users to seats that existed in the past. This approach uses continuity as a justification for expansion: restoring past levels of access to seating by building more space for seats for the larger population of people. When libraries have a long history, as many do, then a continuity story might be the most appropriate way to encourage audience engagement and tell prospective donors how their money will sustain the impact of the past for the library users of today. In other situations, there is no clear past or precedent to draw upon to set current or future access levels, and so we must discover more about what is needed.

The Discovery Story

The discovery story can occur when a library looks outward into the community. Let's imagine that library staff are working on a proposal to collaborate with a neighborhood community center. The first meetings go very well until the issue of transportation arises. Discovery begins as the library staff and center volunteers look at maps together. They see that the library and the center are about five miles apart, and to make that journey, children and families would have to walk on streets with no sidewalks, or take a trip on public transportation that involves transfers from bus to train to bus. The team begins to understand why children in this neighborhood are less likely to have library cards than those in other parts of the city. This discovery leads to a plan for mobile library card sign-up, as well as input to the local transit district to consider changes to bus routes.

Discovery stories can also involve the library looking inward. Imagine a library that has been doing a series of very well-attended programs. However, staff notice that program attendance is not translating into more library cards or higher circulation. People seem to be coming in for the programs and leaving without connecting with the array of opportunities that the library offers. Why? To discover more, they decide to survey people as they come in for the next program to learn more about what they like—and don't like—about the library. The survey results lead to a series of discoveries: First, those who attend programs are from higher-income neighborhoods and are buying more books themselves, so they are attending programs more but borrowing less than they buy. Second, based on cardholder records, those not attending programs are coming from lower-income neighborhoods. Statistically, they are coming in at times when programs are not offered, often the last hours of the day, to borrow materials or do homework. So the programs are not aligning with the timing of lower-income community members' availability, and the library has more work to do to build more equitable opportunities for all.

Discovery stories can center on questions of why or how something about the library is working or not working (see figure 3.4). The discovery structure comes from Roland Barthes's comprehensive semiotic analysis of a novella, an attempt to understand the ways that meaning drives a narrative. Barthes's "enigma" or hermeneutic code is a narrative structure organized around a sense of intrigue or curiosity (Barthes 1974). A discovery narrative structure centers on suspense and discovery, intrigue and information, and curiosity and satisfaction. It feels like a mystery story, where the audience follows the investigation of a detective as they come to understand "whodunit" or what happened. The emotional experience is that of suspense and intrigue, followed by the satisfaction of coming to understand the resolution. This narrative structure appears in library storytimes when a librarian asks a young audience: "What do you think will happen next?"

The enigma structure of suspense and surprise or satisfaction may be an overarching story theme or a micro-structure that is repeated many times within a narrative that combines insights from various data sets. Data stories may have a discovery structure that generates suspense about what will happen to the character-as-data over time, in a setting that includes a puzzle or problem, or through a plot that invites the audience to engage in the mystery of the unknown and delight in coming to know and understand the solution.

Just like mysteries, discovery stories can be very exciting. For example, grant funds and library staffing turnover can sometimes unexpectedly accumulate a budget surplus. Discovering that there is more money in a fund than was previously thought is often a great way to instigate and easily justify a special project. The suspense for the audience is: "What should we do with the money?" And the narrative progresses with an aim to convey excitement, the project's potential, and the possibility of what happens next and the impact it could have.

Discovery stories can also be tragic, as when it turns out that recent changes to the provision of public transit service have created new challenges for certain

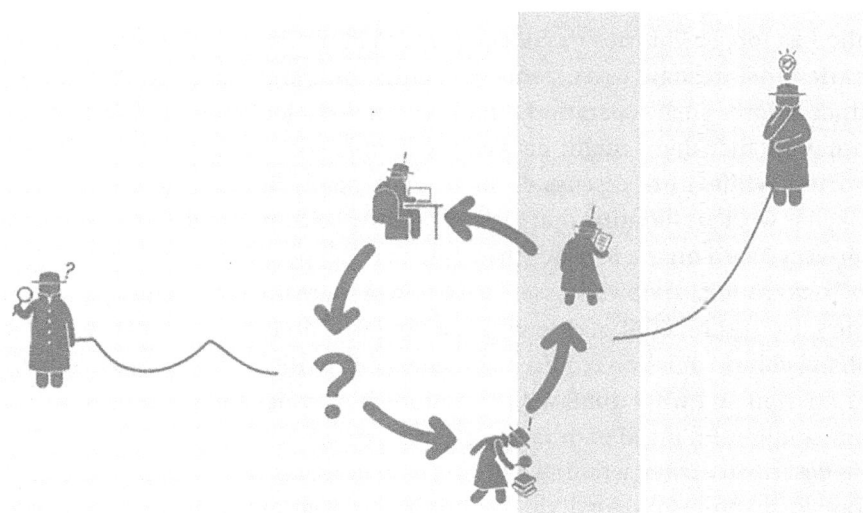

FIGURE 3.4
The discovery story

Source: Xinhui Hu

neighborhoods, perhaps creating new book deserts. Book deserts are places where there is no affordable way for children and families to access reading materials consistently (Neuman and Moland 2019). The concept of a book desert relates to the concept of food deserts, places where there is no consistent access to affordable fresh produce. Whether joyful or tragic, many discovery stories result from combining two kinds of data, like information about poverty and geography, or library users/cardholders and neighborhood.

Donor Funding as a Discovery Story
Another way to sustain engagement is to tell a story where the audience experiences the emotions of discovering something new. Let's imagine a situation where, despite the promise of a big donation, a new library building was not built. Why would that happen? Perhaps there was an unwelcome discovery in which the donor was found to have ties to pro-censorship activist groups. The motivation behind the donation included increasing surveillance and making the library building more invasive of users' privacy, including what they chose to read. This ulterior motive directly contravenes the library value of intellectual freedom and, unfortunately, is not an extreme example—recent legislation in

Idaho has forced libraries to police access to books in the adult-only areas of libraries and, in some cases, refuse to admit children in smaller libraries that cannot enforce such separation (Pfannenstiel and Maldonado 2024). It is easy to imagine that there might be wealthy donors who support surveillance in libraries. While a full discussion of surveillance is beyond the scope of this book, it is worth reiterating that libraries should be committed to the protection of privacy based on the bedrock principle that "all people, regardless of origin, age, background, or views, possess a right to privacy and confidentiality in their library use" (ALA 2006). A case where a potential donor's motivations conflict with the library's mission requires a broader community conversation to identify that mission and what unbiased protections it provides for all patrons. At that point, another financial path forward must be found.

As described earlier, a failing building with heroic donors who save the day is a transformation story. Justifying a building renovation that restores space for users is a continuity story. Learning that a potential donor's intentions go against the ethics of librarianship is a discovery story. Classic narrative structures offer an intuitive way for some thinkers to develop stories. But data-centric thinkers may need a different approach. The next section will center data-focused plot development.

Data-Focused Plot Development

In addition to the three classic narrative structures just discussed, another way to think about the process of developing data stories is to consider the order of events in the story. The *plot* is the action, meaning what changes, has changed, or should change over time as the audience comes to understand the meaning of the data it is compiling. Practically, storytelling is a chronological art form, and every data story will occur as a sequence—involving struggles or suspense—that the audience follows. Data story plots are often simple in comparison to TV shows, movies, or folklore, but they serve the same kinds of purposes. A plot shows the audience not only what happens over time but also how actions relate to other information in the story, such as the motivations of the different characters in the story.

The plot is also what carries the momentum of the middle of the story. The setting usually carries the beginning, and change in (or the revelation of) the meaning of the data carries the ending. The plot is what comes in between. For a data storyteller, building a plot in the middle of the story requires some kind of strategy to organize the information and keep the audience emotionally involved. Table 3.2 summarizes some examples of common plot strategies on the left and the corresponding applications to what data analysis may show on the right.

Change over Time

Change over time is perhaps the most intuitive strategy for building a plot; it involves tracing the change over time in the data or comparisons between two sets of data. This strategy is useful for indicating what changed, how it changed, and what can be known about that change. Examples might be year-to-year comparisons of library circulation records, which become quite interesting when external forces like a worldwide pandemic disrupt patterns of everyday life and library borrowing. Change over time is used to describe past events and their outcomes. Organizing data with a change over time can also help libraries make future projections based on past events.

Comparison or Parallel Changes

Comparison or parallel changes is another plot strategy, which puts related sets of data points or trends into dialogue with each other. This exchange can serve to highlight differences, similarities, or the gaps between different kinds of data. A library example would be a comparison between circulation at different branches, especially if there seem to be dramatic declines in borrowing at one location and dramatic increases at another. Focusing on those differences might

TABLE 3.2
Plot Strategies and Applications for Data Stories

PLOT STRATEGY	APPLICATION TO DATA
Change over time	When change is the most important meaning of the story
Comparison or parallel changes	When two types of data have some correlation or relationship such that one changes or seems to change in relation to the other
Inquiry process	When the audience needs to understand the data analysis and how analysis leads to new information
Shift in audience's understanding	When evidence derived from new data contradicts commonly held ideas

lead to questions about building maintenance and the relative attractiveness of the two branch libraries. Or it might lead to questions about community car ownership, parking, barriers to walking or biking, or other transportation or transit questions.

Parallel approaches can also help to emphasize correlations across situations that are difficult to understand, such as when there are major unexplained drops in usage across a large library system. This kind of comparison is particularly effective when the teller invites the audience to join in understanding a complex phenomenon. In the case of unexplained usage drops, there may be multiple factors. A strict causal explanation might be difficult or impossible to establish. Libraries must contend with difficult realities, often leading to larger questions about social context.

The Inquiry Process

When the audience needs to understand the data analysis and how this analysis leads to new information, the plot should be structured as an inquiry process. This plot captures a sequential process of moving from ignorance to knowledge. For example, inquiry is a great frame for presenting library survey results to an audience of decision-makers. The plot is organized by a series of questions that build on each other, such as how library patrons' attitudes correlate with income levels, neighborhoods, and schools attended. This series of questions and answers provides insight into what users think of the library as it relates to their socioeconomic status. The *inquiry process* plot works best when the data show clear causation or at least substantial correlations. When presenting survey results, it might seem logical to start with community demographics. This will work well if there are clear patterns showing a correlation between, for example, demographic data about home ownership and library usage. However, this will not work well if the findings are not clear; the audience will become confused and may be unwilling to join in the inquiry process if the findings are muddled.

Consider which findings will engage the audience's curiosity right away. Logically organizing survey findings for a data storytelling audience will mean stepping back from the order in which the questions were asked in the survey. The audience needs to be motivated by a sense of curiosity. Inquiry processes are especially important to check with rehearsal audiences, as it can be hard to sequence questions and imagine what others might ask as they hear initial answers.

Shift in Audience's Understanding

The *shift in audience's understanding* strategy is appropriate when a story will present new information that contradicts popular opinion. With this kind of plot, the data story reveals information that changes the audience's understanding. For example, it might seem that the library has nothing to do with environmental activism, but the efficiency of its building systems—from electronic door openers or foot traffic trackers to heating, cooling, and humidity regulation—means that the library does have a measurable environmental impact. Similarly, decisions like whether to increase parking or to advertise alternatives, such as public transit or parking lots a block away, have implications for the environment that should be considered along with other factors. This plot strategy works best when the audience's understanding is insufficiently informed or is missing a bigger-picture understanding.

A Note on Plot

Plot is more than just a sequence, although the aforementioned strategies all relate to sequence. It is more complex than causality, although many plots do include causally related events. The audience hears a story's sequence, but they will interpret for themselves what they believe to be causally connected or merely sequentially correlated (Polletta 2006). Honest data storytelling, like the best tradition of honest library storytelling, cites its sources carefully (Hearne 1993). Plots can also be difficult to contain, especially when an audience infers causality (factual or implied) because this might make their retellings more dramatic or exaggerated than is strictly accurate (Rosling et al. 2018). On the other hand, many data sets are opaque to public audiences without some additional information, so library data storytellers play a vital role in making data accessible. If the data doesn't lend itself clearly to one of these plots, there are other ways to create a story from data. It may be helpful to work on an iterative revision of the data into information and knowledge tempered by wisdom.

S-DIKW Iterative Revision: From Data to Story ──────

Iterative revision means a process of refinement that generates multiple versions (or iterations) of a story until we have created an effective version of it. DIKW stands for "data, information, knowledge, and wisdom." The DIKW pyramid appears regularly in information studies textbooks as one of the most fundamental, most widely recognized and adopted models for understanding information conceptually (Rowley 2007). T. S. Eliot (1962) is often credited with inspiring the term *DIKW* with his 1934 poem "The Rock": "Where is the wisdom that we have lost in knowledge? / Where is the knowledge that we have lost in information?" DIKW has alternatively been called the information hierarchy, the knowledge hierarchy, or the wisdom hierarchy. While there have been multiple ways to understand and visualize DIKW, the set and sequence of four levels remains the same: data, information, knowledge, and wisdom.

The S-DIKW framework (S for storytelling) adapts DIKW for practical applications in data storytelling (McDowell 2021). Each level of the framework relates to the human abilities to derive stories from data, to interpret data with context as information stories, to take action based on those information stories, and to enact wisdom based on what we know. The S-DIKW framework has four levels:

- S-Data: Basis of information in story
- S-Information: Data interpretation with context as story
- S-Knowledge: Actionable information in story
- S-Wisdom: Which story to tell when, how, to whom, and more

Each level interacts with the one next to it. For example, we work from data as the basis of the information in a story, but the way the information is delivered may require rechecking the data to ensure accuracy. Similarly, the knowledge of what action to take next may require clarifying the representation of the information. Complex data storytelling needs supporting data visualization. The S-DIKW framework can be used to support the translation of raw data into a data story for presentation, as shown in table 3.3.

This translation starts at the level of data, perhaps with a simple visualization like a chart representing an insight extracted from raw data. Then the visualization (or other representation of data) is enriched with new elements as it ascends into the levels of information, knowledge, and (ideally) wisdom. When the enrichment reaches the level of knowledge or wisdom, the data has been converted into a powerful data story. S-Knowledge here is derived from the narrower definition of actionable information (Rowley 2007) rather than concepts like "knowledge management" or "knowledge commons." The definition of S-Wisdom is only partial, but it provides a launching point for information fields to more actively and deliberately grapple with wisdom as a concept (McDowell 2024).

TABLE 3.3
S-DIKW Framework for Iterative Revision

S-DIKW FRAMEWORK	TEXTUAL AND VISUAL ELEMENTS
S-Data	Choose the visualization type, focusing on a problem/issue that the audience will follow.
S-Information	Add textual and graphic context describing the initial situation before the problem occurs.
S-Knowledge	Define the enigma, disclose what happens, explain how/if the problem is solved and what to do next.
S-Wisdom	Tailor the visualization to the type of audience and explain/show why taking action matters.

Adapted from Lo Duca and McDowell, 2025.

S-Data: Extracting and Representing Relevant Facts

Choosing data points depends on the purpose of the story. Before representing data in narrative or visuals, data storytellers should ensure that they have permission to represent them. In addition, data should be of high quality and should respect data privacy policies (Dykes 2020). While it may be difficult given pervasive social biases, data should be as fair and non-discriminatory as possible (Benjamin 2019). Data that represents people deserves additional consideration so that it causes no harm to anyone it represents.

Extracting Relevant Facts from Data

In applying the S-DIKW framework to data storytelling, *S-Data* is the visual representation of a relevant fact or facts extracted from data. A relevant fact is something worth telling through a story, something that people will want to know. Transforming data into S-Data means building the main scene of the data story, which should be represented by a clear chart.

Various data analysis techniques can be applied to extract relevant facts from data, such as descriptive statistics, inferential statistics, data mining, and machine learning. These techniques enable the identification of patterns relationships, and trends in the data, making them informative to an audience. In his book *Seeing What Others Don't*, Gary Klein (2013) identifies four main strategies to identify a relevant fact: connections, coincidences, curiosity, and contradictions. The *connection* strategy involves identifying the main points of data and then connecting them to identify a story. The *coincidence* strategy involves searching for repeated events in data. To identify whether a repeated event is a coincidence, isolated events should be ignored while looking for longer-term patterns that suggest a relationship. The *curiosity* strategy searches for a wide range of phenomena in data, including outliers, missing data, data gaps across time or space, sudden shifts or trends, unexpected patterns, and more. When something curious is noted in data, new questions are raised, and hence the underlying factors contributing to the observed patterns may need to be explored. Finally, the *contradiction* strategy searches for two or more beliefs or pieces of evidence that conflict with data, creating an inconsistency. According to Klein, to extract insight from contradictions, a skeptical mindset should be used to approach data. Unlike a coincidence-based approach, where repetition may indicate patterns, a contradiction-based strategy seeks out seemingly conflicting events.

Representing Relevant Facts

Depending on the type of data being analyzed, different techniques can effectively represent data visually. For quantitative data, common chart types include bar charts, line charts, scatter plots, and histograms. Qualitative data is often represented using charts like pie charts, stacked bar charts, and word clouds. These visual representations provide a concise and intuitive means of conveying information, facilitating comprehension and interpretation. Other books describe data analysis in more detail, but for our purposes, the first step in creating a data story is choosing how to represent data. Table 3.4 provides suggestions, although librarians can leverage their imagination and expertise to build new and more creative types of charts.

For example, imagine that a library has seen slow but steady declines in donations over the past five years. This trend could be represented as a line chart supplemented by the raw data of the highest donation amount—five years ago—and the lowest dollar amount from the current year. A question from a recent survey might result in a bar chart of responses as to why people do or do not donate to the library. A series of choropleth maps might indicate where donors live and, by sharing each map sequentially, could show where people most or least likely to donate have lived over the past five years.

TABLE 3.4
Recommended Techniques to Represent Data

DATA TO REPRESENT	DESCRIPTION	SUGGESTED CHARTS
A single piece of data	A single number representing critical information	• Big Number (BAN) • Donut Chart • 100% Stacked Bar Chart • Waffle Chart
Trend	The behavior of an entity over time	• Line Chart • Small Multiple Line Chart • Stacked Area Chart • Stacked Column Chart
Outcomes of a survey or a questionnaire	Responses to questions contained in a survey or a questionnaire	• Stacked Bar Chart • Column Chart • Multiple Bar Charts
Distribution	Spread of values across a data set, indicating how frequently different values occur	• Histogram • Pyramid • Box Plot
Relationship	Association, connection, or correlation between different entities to identify patterns, trends, and dependencies	• Scatterplot • Bubble Chart • Heatmap
Spatial information	The behavior of an entity over space	• Choropleth Map • Dot Density Map • Proportional Symbol Map • Heatmap
Parts of a whole	The components contributing to the entirety of a system, object, or concept, especially when the sum of all components must be 100%	• Pie Chart • 100% Stacked Bar Chart • Multiple Waffle Chart • Donut Chart
Comparison	Similarities and differences between multiple entities to establish relationships and distinctions	• Bar Chart • Column Chart • Slope Graph • Dumbbell Chart • Table

Generated collaboratively with Dr. Angelica Lo Duca, Università di Pisa, Italy

S-Information: Tailoring the Data to Audience for a Story

The next step in the S-DIKW framework is *S-Information*. Turning data into information means tailoring the data and visualization to a story form for the intended audience. This step sets the scene by presenting an initial situation—a reduction in donations—along with how donations have changed by neighborhood. S-Information has two main considerations: the amount of information and what the audience already knows (or does not know).

The amount of information depends on the type of audience. Audience types can be grouped into three categories with some intersection: the general public, executives, and professionals. The *general public* may have little or no previous knowledge of the data, so the key tactic is to avoid overwhelming them with too much information. The focus should be on presenting the most relevant facts, visually and engagingly. *Executives* are typically high-level decision-makers in organizations who rely on data for insights to make challenging choices. They often have limited time and need concise information that is accurate and clear, so they need key findings, trends, and recommendations. *Professionals* consist of individuals with specific domain expertise or professional background who have a deeper understanding of data and require more analytical information. Data stories for professionals should explain the method of data analysis, assumptions, and limitations, so that they are well-positioned to communicate their expert insights to executives. Table 3.5 provides some recommendations about what general amount and type of information to represent based on the audience type.

To convey data in story form, the data should not overwhelm the audience. It is a classic error to attempt to include too much data in a story. In the earlier example of declining library donations over the past five years, the public will likely need just the line chart (the amount of decline over time). Executives may need the line chart and the bar chart (survey responses indicating why people do or do not donate). Professionals, especially advancement and communications or public relations professionals, will benefit from the line chart, the bar chart, and the choropleth map (neighborhoods where donors live), so they can understand as much as possible about the analysis of the problem and which neighborhoods give the most and the least.

The selection of a data representation technique for S-Information requires a consideration of what will provide the intended audience with new data and information to support its process of meaning-making and insight. While it is

TABLE 3.5
Recommended Data Representations Based on Intended Audience

AUDIENCE TYPE	REQUIREMENTS	WHAT TO REPRESENT
General public	Understand data	An appealing overview of insights
Executives	High-level overview of data trends to aid strategic decision-making	Highlight critical metrics and recent trends that might influence future outcomes
Professionals	Detailed insights to understand the phenomenon behind data	Add numbers, statistics, and helpful information to understand insights deeply and communicate them effectively

impossible to know everything about every audience, this decision can be at least partially discerned by practicing with rehearsal audiences who represent the target audience type. Practicing stories with rehearsal audiences allows storytellers to tailor S-Information to the information needs of the intended audience. Once an audience is informed, then they may acquire knowledge about what to do.

S-Knowledge: Transforming Data into a Meaningful Story

S-Knowledge is information enriched with context, so that an audience can understand the data as information that prompts them to action. If the data is represented in a clear visual, then the S-Knowledge step means adding captions, annotations, or symbols to that visualization that will reinforce the meaning of the data. If the data is narrated, then the S-Knowledge step is the main takeaway or even the moral of the story, in practical terms. In both cases, this revision process involves indicating in clear terms a knowledge of what should be done and one (or more) examples of how to take action. For example, library leadership may learn about which local festivals or events they might target with a campaign by considering specific neighborhoods, their donation levels, and of course the income levels in those neighborhoods.

Drawing on the earlier example, data showing a downward trend in year-to-year donations may be prepared as a line chart (*S-Data*). Then, for sharing with professionals and executives, the data is transformed to indicate the scale of the resulting funding deficits over time (*S-Information*). Next, the data is enriched with an accompanying narration and annotations to support a proposal for what action to take, such as launching a new fundraising campaign targeting neighborhoods with relatively high income levels and low donation levels (*S-Knowledge*).

S-Wisdom: Bigger Picture and Next Steps

S-Wisdom involves guiding the audience toward the bigger picture they should consider when taking action. The story can include a contextual explanation of what is a wise or just actionable outcome. For example, if the five-year donation decline is the result of a significant economic recession in the region, then a fundraising campaign might be an unwise response. Instead, the library might work to see how collaborations with other community organizations that are also suffering from the economic situation can pool resources to increase their positive impact for the community.

Sometimes S-Wisdom means supplementing the existing data with a speculative visualization of what a continued trend might mean for the future. Most often, this speculation will be added to the data visualization as annotations or an accompanying narration that explains the bigger-picture implications. For example, a library with a downward donation trend, but one located in a region with economic stability or growth, might benefit from an exploratory visualization of what that continued decline in donations would mean in another five years. This visualization could help emphasize the importance of launching a fundraising campaign as soon as possible, so as to reverse the trend and increase library donations over the long term. This visualization could be accompanied by narrating what specific benefits would result from increasing donations to help motivate the audience to take the necessary actions.

Using S-DIKW Iterative Revision to Structure Data Story Presentations

Data stories can be layered into presentations with complex structures if the audience's experience is at the heart of the effort. A good presentation can tell multiple stories, interweaving stories of people's real experiences with information that helps make broader sense of individual stories. Data stories can interweave narrative structures with different data-focused plots. The ultimate result of a data storytelling process is a presentation that keeps the audience engaged and interested throughout. The key elements can be organized and remixed in many ways: for example, by including at least one story of a real person; showing how data is relevant to this story and to what should happen; and a proposal for what to plan or do next.

Here's an example of a data storytelling presentation structure for a group of executives—specifically, a public library's board of trustees—based on the dwindling library donations example from the S-DIKW iterative revision process. Iterative revision starts from data, but notice that the sequence of the iterative revision steps will likely vary from the sequence of the final storytelling presentation. This is because it is more effective to begin with a story about who benefits from the library than to begin with data.

- *S-Information: Opening story* about a person who benefits from the library, named with enthusiastic permission or anonymized/amalgamated from multiple people. For example, imagine a child who received a free book through the summer reading program, which was supported by donations from the Friends of the Library.
- *S-Data: Current data* from your library, such as data about donations in the current year (chart) and in which neighborhoods donors live (choropleth map).
- *S-Data: Historical data* showing trends over time, such as data about donation levels in the previous few years (line chart or series of choropleth maps).
- *S-Knowledge: Story* about the data, including how to make use of this information as knowledge to take action. For example, the story could suggest:
    Change (transformation) through a new fundraising campaign.
    Remaining stable (continuity) by sustaining relationships with current donors.
    Gathering more data to decide what should be done next (discovery) by creating a new survey of patrons, both donors and non-donors.
- *S-Information and S-Wisdom: Demographic data* about the community, representing current or future patrons and how the community context makes the course of action a wise one.
- *S-Wisdom:* Return to the *opening story*, a child who benefits from the summer reading program, but now with more information about the current state of the library and how many children could or should benefit in the future.

- *S-Wisdom: Listening.* Conclude with inviting the board to give input, start a discussion, or hold a vote on how to proceed in light of the story presented. The best storytelling situations incorporate interaction, so that the audience and teller have opportunities to trade places. Great storytellers are exceptional listeners.

There are some implicit strategies here, like hooking the audience quickly with a story of a real person and then circling back to that story by the ending. The exploration of relevant data and information should be organized so that each insight builds to the next. These elements could be remixed and presented in any order that makes sense for the audience. If the audience has enough time and space to fully process, absorb, and understand the data story and its implications, then any number of creative presentation structures will work. Any data storyteller can bring their own voice, knowledge, and personality to a presentation that remains accurate and honest. By doing so, the chances of engaging the audience increase dramatically, as sharing insights in one's own voice is the most effective way to demonstrate diligence, sincerity, and a desire to impart information.

Story Is Not Neutral

From a critical perspective, it is important to note that story, like data, is not neutral. Histories of libraries are not neutral, and libraries are not neutral. In fact, libraries have not always been welcoming to all people despite their stated missions, and so critical data storytelling perspectives are necessary. Advocacy alone will not ensure equity because not all forms of exclusion have been addressed equitably. Despite years of conversation about social justice in libraries, including those about critical library instruction specifically, efforts to increase the visibility of stories of people of color are routinely undermined by unexamined or recalcitrant commitments to whiteness. In examining how to indicate that diversity will be respected, Jennifer Ferretti tells a story about posting a sign outside a conference session: "Do not enter this room if you don't believe the narratives of people of color." The sign then appeared on the social network Twitter (now X), where a white librarian deemed it "hostile" and "unwelcoming." While this is also an object lesson about story and context, it is emblematic of the ways that whiteness trains white people to assert themselves as the center of every conversation. Bias, discrimination, and microaggressions lead to brilliant people leaving the profession. It will take more work to move from critical data storytelling to achieving real change in the "power relations between library colleagues" (Ferretti 2020, 137). Real change will not come without centering BIPOC voices in librarianship. Most data has indicated that recruitment efforts to diversify the profession have only maintained, not increased, diversity, with some years even seeing decreases. (Muller 2012). Based on data from 2021, the Public Library Association's first report on staffing and diversity demonstrated that "Black, Indigenous, and people of color (BIPOC) are underrepresented in the library workforce, while white people—and white women in particular—are overrepresented" (Public Library Association 2022). Equitable story-building is only possible by being conscious of these ongoing troubles in our field and working for change.

Other fields have moved ahead in some areas, particularly in ways to teach and learn about race. In a fascinating study of creating counter-storytelling communities in social justice education, Lee Anne Bell (2010) defines four categories of story related to making change:

- Stock
- Concealed
- Resistance
- Emerging/Transforming

Stock stories are those that sustain and replicate systemic injustices. They might seem "normal" but are rife with the bias they perpetuate in their retelling. *Concealed stories* are not told so openly. They "embody the teeming, unruly and contradictory stories that leak out from the margins." Typically, these stories are "eclipsed by stock stories" that "colonize the limelight" (43). Concealed stories are revealed on the way to resistance. *Resistance stories* are about showing injustice and advocating for fairness, equity, and change. "These are stories that narrate the persistent and ingenious ways people, both ordinary and famous, resist racism and challenge the stock stories that support it in order to fight for more equal and inclusive social arrangements" (61). Finally, *Emerging/Transforming stories* build on concealed and resistance stories. They enable people to "enact continuing critique and resistance to stock stories" and "envision alternatives to the status quo and generate strategies to realize our visions for racial equity in classrooms, schools and communities" (75).

Because some aspects of library advocacy are inevitably enmeshed with systemic injustices, we need this social justice framework when thinking about the critical aspects of library advocacy narratives. Even before getting to the different ways to structure interpretations of data as story, we need to be aware that stories are always doing some kind of work. They are contributing to maintaining the status quo, or they are revealing things that have been concealed. Stories show why injustices matter and how things can be better. A social justice approach to story provides another way of thinking about how informational and emotional content are intertwined in data stories for library advocacy, particularly when it intersects or overlaps with community advocacy.

Counter-Narratives

The data shows that groups of people, especially Black, Indigenous, and People of Color (BIPOC), routinely experience overt and covert hostilities that repeatedly communicate feelings of being unwelcome in libraries, as patrons and as staff (ALA 2018). Such groups are routinely subject to microaggressions, which are "malignant, yet inconspicuous, messages of inferiority to already marginalized groups" that result in a professional culture which is "exclusionary and hostile to diverse librarians" (LaBossiere and Deese 2020). Similarly, female-presenting trans colleagues have encountered administrators who deny or disbelieve their stories about sexual harassment by patrons (Horner 2022). One aspect of the problem is an inability to listen on the part of colleagues in the dominant or privileged groups. Bell (2010) writes about this phenomenon in workshops as a pattern she has seen again and again:

> An African American woman speaks tearfully about her shock at discovering the degree to which racial advantage and disadvantage are constructed, newly recognizing ways that her own life has been affected. Before she can finish, a white participant interrupts and asserts that she too has experienced disadvantage and that the problem is really class, not race. One can feel the entire room hold its collective breath. Clearly this is a crucial moment. Will we move on with the discussion as often happens, smoothing over tension and disagreement? Instead, one of the facilitators quietly asks the white participant to repeat what she heard her African-American colleagues say; when she cannot do so, it becomes clear that she had tuned out the first speaker. (Bell 2010, 103)

Bell goes on to describe how the group fully acknowledges the first speaker before moving on. By slowing down and making space to understand how anecdotes can be used to overwrite and stop listening to another person's experience, workshops can reach a turning point where the participants are able to

> listen carefully while examining how racial positionality impacts their ability to listen to and learn from one another, to own their ability to either collude in or interrupt such practices, and to explore more deeply patterns we typically take for granted or pass over that enable racism to continue. (Bell 2010, 104)

Thinking critically about power and power structures also means preparing to intervene when the usual exclusions operate. Everyone is responsible for being an "active bystander" when colleagues face discrimination and exclusion (Cooke 2017).

Conclusion

Data stories can be carefully constructed—with words, visuals, captions, and more—to reinforce and reiterate the most important numbers, measures, or statistics and imprint these on the audience's mind. Respect for audiences, however, means connecting with real people—individuals, focus groups, community groups, and more—to better understand what they care about, what their stories are, and what they are likely to remember from a library data story. Audiences have limited attention, and it is wise to start from a place of compassion for those limits in developing a data story.

There are many good ways to construct good data stories. The three approaches here—classic narrative structures, data-focused plots, and S-DIKW iterative revision—align with common approaches to story-building among information professionals: story-focused, data-focused, and iterative revision from data to story. There are also many combinations of these approaches, as well as additional ways of developing data stories. These three approaches offer ways of crafting narratives, either by building on knowledge of the story, a plot based on data, or through a process of revision, from data to story. No story is completely crafted without its audience, and the next chapter describes why audiences matter, due either to their familiarity with or knowledge of the data or to their attitudes.

FURTHER READINGS

Bowles, Meg, Catherine Burns, Jenifer Hixson, Sarah Austin Jenness, and Kate Tellers. 2022. *How to Tell a Story: The Essential Guide to Memorable Storytelling from the Moth.* Crown.

> For storytellers hoping to add personal elements and hone the emotional elements of library data stories; especially the chapters on structuring stories and heightening emotions.

Cooke, Nicole A. 2016. "Counter-Storytelling in the LIS Curriculum." In *Perspectives on Libraries as Institutions of Human Rights and Social Justice*, vol. 41: 331–48. Emerald Group Publishing. https://doi.org/10.1108/S0065-283020160000041014.

> For those seeking to create compelling experiences of narrative that include marginalized perspectives to increase equity and cultural competence.

Lipman, Doug. 1999. *Improving Your Storytelling: Beyond the Basics for All Who Tell Stories in Work or Play.* August House.

> For storytellers with some experience who want to more fully embody storytelling presence and dynamics.

Spaulding, Amy E. 2011. *The Art of Storytelling: Telling Truths Through Telling Stories.* Scarecrow.

> For those hoping to understand more about the tradition of storytelling in libraries as it intersects with folklore traditions and what can be learned from old stories for structuring new ones.

REFERENCES

Adichie, Chimamanda Ngozi. 2009. "The Danger of a Single Story" [TED talk]. July. www.ted.com/talks/chimamanda_ngozi_adichie_the_danger_of_a_single_story?language=en.

ALA American Library Association. 2006. "Privacy: An Interpretation of the Library Bill of Rights." Advocacy, Legislation & Issues. www.ala.org/advocacy/intfreedom/librarybill/interpretations/privacy.

ALA. 2018. "Hateful Conduct in Libraries: Supporting Library Workers and Patrons." Advocacy, Legislation & Issues. www.ala.org/advocacy/hatefulconduct.

Association of Public & Land-Grant Universities. n.d. "The Value and Benefit of Public Universities." www.aplu.org/our-work/4-policy-and-advocacy/publicuvalues/.

Barthes, Roland. 1974. *S/Z.* Hill and Wang.

Bell, Lee Anne. 2010. *Storytelling for Social Justice: Connecting Narrative and the Arts in Antiracist Teaching.* 2nd edition. Routledge. https://doi.org/10.4324/9780203852231.

Benjamin, Ruha. 2019. *Race after Technology: Abolitionist Tools for the New Jim Code.* Polity.

Campbell, Joseph. 1949. *The Hero with a Thousand Faces.* Pantheon Books.

Cooke, Nicole A. 2014. "Pushing Back from the Table: Fighting to Maintain My Voice as a Pre-tenure Minority Female in the White Academy." *Polymath: An Interdisciplinary Journal of Arts & Sciences* 4, no. 2.

Cooke, Nicole A. 2017. "Librarians as Active Bystanders: Centering Social Justice in LIS Practice." Atla. www.atla.com/webinar/librarians-as-active-bystanders-centering-social-justice-in-lis-practice/.

Cooke, Nicole A. 2019. "Impolite Hostilities and Vague Sympathies: Academia as a Site of Cyclical Abuse." *Journal of Education for Library and Information Science* 60, no. 3: 223–30. https://doi.org/10.3138/jelis.2019-0005.

Dykes, Brent. 2020. *Effective Data Storytelling: How to Drive Change with Data, Narrative and Visuals.* John Wiley and Sons.

Eliot, T. S. 1962. *The Waste Land, and Other Poems.* Harcourt, Brace, Jovanovich.

Ferretti, Jennifer A. 2020. "Building a Critical Culture: How Critical Librarianship Falls Short in the Workplace." *Communications in Information Literacy* 14, no. 1. https://doi.org/10.15760/comminfolit.2020.14.1.10.

Hearne, Betsy. 1993. "Cite the Source: Reducing Cultural Chaos in Picture Books, Part One." *School Library Journal* 39, no. 7 (July): 22–27.

Horner, Katie. 2022. "We Can Do Better—Best (and Worst) Practices for Managers Responding to Sexual Harassment Claims." *Public Libraries Online, A Publication of the Public Library Association* (blog). January 19. https://publiclibrariesonline.org/2022/01/we-can-do-better-best-and-worst-practices-for-managers-responding-to-sexual-harassment-claims/.

Hurley, David A., Sarah R. Kostelecky, and Lori Townsend. 2022. *Cultural Humility.* American Library Association.

Jenkins, Christine. 1995. "The Strength of the Inconspicuous Youth Services Librarians, the American Library Association, and Intellectual Freedom for the Young, 1939–1955." https://research.ebsco.com/linkprocessor/plink?id=091bba40-adbd-3e7b-be6e-6774f63b9398.

Klein, Gary A. 2013. *Seeing What Others Don't: The Remarkable Ways We Gain Insights*. PublicAffairs.

LaBossiere, Tarica, and Abby Deese. 2020. "Keeping Up with . . . Microaggressions." Association of College & Research Libraries. March 17. www.ala.org/acrl/publications/keeping_up_with/microaggressions.

Lo Duca, Angelica, and Kate McDowell. 2025. "Using the S-DIKW Framework to Transform Data Visualization into Data Storytelling." *Journal of the Association for Information Science and Technology* 76, no. 5: 803–18. https://doi.org/10.1002/asi.24973.

McDowell, Kate. 2021. "Storytelling Wisdom: Story, Information, and DIKW." *Journal of the Association for Information Science and Technology* 72, no. 10 (Special issue: "Paradigm Shift in the Field of Information"): 1223–33. https://doi.org/10.1002/asi.24466.

McDowell, Kate. 2024. "Storytelling and/as Misinformation: Storytelling Dynamics and Narrative Structures for Three Cases of COVID-19 Viral Misinformation." In *Everyday Misinformation*. Cambridge University Press. https://hdl.handle.net/2142/117174.

Muller, Karen. 2012. "Librarian Ethnicity." Tools, Publications & Resources. American Library Association. July 11. www.ala.org/tools/librarian-ethnicity.

Neuman, Susan B., and Naomi Moland. 2019. "Book Deserts: The Consequences of Income Segregation on Children's Access to Print." *Urban Education*, 54, no. 1: 126–47. https://doi.org/10.1177/0042085916654525.

Pfannenstiel, Kyle, and Mia Maldonado. 2024. "'We Are Not Getting Rid of Books': How Libraries across Idaho Are Implementing New Materials Law." *Idaho Capital Sun*. July 15. https://idahocapitalsun.com/2024/07/15/we-are-not-getting-rid-of-books-how-libraries-across-idaho-are-implementing-new-materials-law/.

Polletta, Francesca. 2006. *It Was Like a Fever: Storytelling in Protest and Politics*. University of Chicago Press. https://doi.org/10.1177/009430610803700327.

PLA Public Library Association. 2022. "2021 Public Library Staff and Diversity Report: Results from the 2021 PLA Annual Survey." www.ala.org/sites/default/files/pla/content/data/PLA_Staff_Survey_Report_2022.pdf.

Rosling, Hans, with Ola Rosling and Anna Rosling Rönnlund. 2018. *Factfulness: Ten Reasons We're Wrong about the World—and Why Things Are Better Than You Think*. Flatiron Books.

Rowley, Jennifer. 2007. "The Wisdom Hierarchy: Representations of the DIKW Hierarchy." *Journal of Information Science* 33, no. 2: 163–80. https://doi.org/10.1177/0165551506070706.

Sturm, Brian. 2008. "Stonecutter (Indonesia, Japan, China)—ProQuest." *Knowledge Quest* 36, no. 5: 59.

Todorov, Tzvetan, and Arnold Weinstein. 1969. "Structural Analysis of Narrative." *NOVEL: A Forum on Fiction* 3, no. 1: 70–76. https://doi.org/10.2307/1345003.

1. This story also comes from a number of sources that styled it as a "Japanese" story, especially in Andrew Lang's 1903 *The Crimson Fairy Book*, but it is most likely European in origin. For a discussion of related tales and origins, see Victoria Somoff and Nancy Canepa, eds., "Morals and Miracles: The Case of ATU 555, 'The Fisherman and His Wife,'" in *Teaching Fairy Tales* (Wayne State University Press, n.d.), 110–19.

Reaching Audiences

Knowledge, Demographics, and Attitudes

I n fall 2023, I gave a talk to an organization of librarians in Florida, where the state legislature has recently begun to regulate all aspects of public education and where librarians are struggling to reach highly polarized audiences. New laws in Florida and other states around the country are attempting to determine what schools can and cannot teach about issues related to the history of race and racism in the United States, impacting libraries of every type. The changing landscape of this legislation is now documented in two online map-based data trackers, one designed for prospective students looking at colleges (bestcolleges.com/news/anti-dei-legislation-tracker/) and another to cultivate awareness among academia as an industry (chronicle.com/article/here-are-the-states-where-lawmakers-are-seeking-to-ban-colleges-dei-efforts). While these laws are likely unconstitutional based on the First Amendment of the US Constitution, it will take much time—maybe years—to recover the ground lost in freedom of thought from their chilling effect, and it may be more difficult depending on how and whether the US Department of Education leadership continues to change.

At the same time, book challenges and bans in public and school libraries across the nation have led to the highest levels of censorship ever recorded in 2022 and 2023. In some cases, successful book bans have emboldened groups like Moms for Liberty that threaten the very existence of libraries. In 2024, the number of reports declined, but remained higher than pre-2020 numbers; ALA contributes the decline to underreporting, censorship by exclusion, and legislative restrictions (American Library Association 2025).

After my talk to the Florida librarians, I took an hour to discuss the data story-telling challenges posed for public, academic, and other kinds of libraries. The librarians asked about how to avoid conversations with hostile leaders so as to prevent even more damage to equitable services and collections in libraries. Sometimes data stories can support the continuity of services and collections, such as continuing to provide diverse books for and about young people who need to see themselves represented in books. In other cases, the librarians asked about withholding certain data and stories to prevent community leaders with hateful perspectives from further harming vulnerable students and faculty members.

The Florida talk exemplifies the state of libraries across communities in the United States. Today, we face extremely polarized audiences who have points of view based on entirely different understandings of reality and what counts as data. These polarized points of view create deeply challenging storytelling situations that require knowing when to work to reach audiences and when to stop engaging in debates that are meant to damage the credibility of the public sphere. Storytelling requires the teller to "know their audience," but how can we do this if every exchange leads to baiting, debating, and ultimately dehumanizing large groups of people, librarians included? Knowing and reaching your audience is not only a matter of relationships. While experience and connections matter, this kind of knowing cannot be based solely on assumptions about many people based on conversations with a few. In fact, the teller can know and reach audiences in multiple ways, including through rehearsals of stories with people from the audiences we hope to reach.

This chapter explores three ways to understand audiences by investigating their knowledge, demographics, and attitudes. Critical approaches to library advocacy storytelling require respecting audiences while also respecting libraries and their mission. Before delving into how to reach audiences, revisiting the dynamic storytelling triangle can reveal some of the social dynamics that influence audiences' reception of library data stories.

Connecting Audiences, Tellers, and Stories

Revisiting the Expanded Storytelling Triangle

In librarianship, we seek compelling narratives not for their own sake but because of the groups they can reach, the audiences they can connect with, and the retelling they can inspire. Storytelling occurs in a dynamic relationship between the teller, the audience, and the story itself, represented by a triangle. A six-part triangle represents the dynamics at play (figure 4.1) and explains why some stories succeed and others fail.

An expanded storytelling triangle includes three dynamic relationships: those between teller and story, between audience and story, and between teller and audience. *Between teller and story* is a relationship based on how the teller came to know the story and why they are choosing to tell it. Audiences are aware of this relationship, and so communicating something about your experience or expertise is important when telling a library data story. Data that demonstrates patterns can be partly supported by anecdotes based on experience. While a library data story should not be purely anecdotal, and entirely based on individual experience or one-time situations, if anecdotes align with evidence, then they can reinforce the validity of the data. The validity of the claims made about data depends in part on whether the audience trusts the teller to tell this story, which may require explaining one's expertise. Offering information to

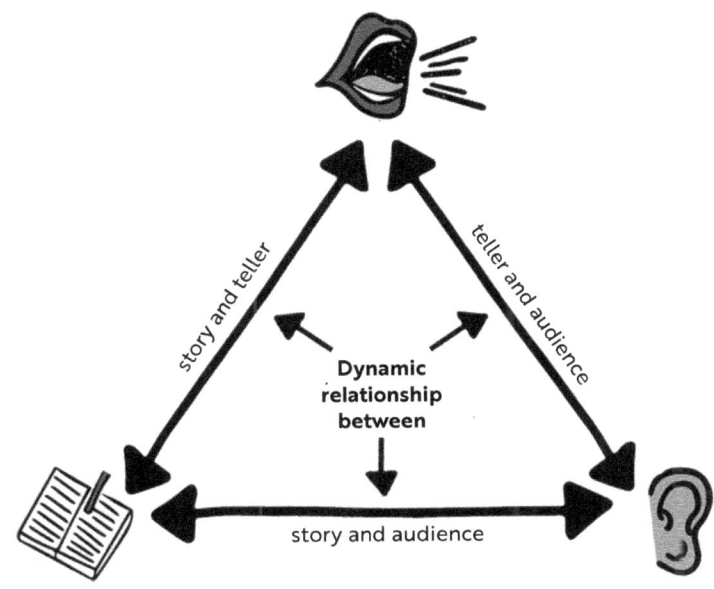

FIGURE 4.1
The expanded storytelling triangle

Credit: Adapted from figure 1.1, which was created by Hilary Pope.

the audience about how you came to the analysis and how it relates to everyday professional practice can help the audience see and understand the relationship between teller and story.

Between audience and story is a relationship that is only partly under the teller's control. Tellers should be watching for audience reactions like eye contact, laughter, sighs, gasps, facial expressions, (or emojis in online contexts) that reveal how the audience is receiving the story. Body language indicating audience engagement, such as nodding or leaning forward to listen, is easily distinguished from signals of disengagement like fidgeting or the blank expression of a person staring at something unrelated on a screen. Seasoned presenters can even read the silence in a room, feeling the difference between silence that signals an intense form of listening and silence that feels cold and disinterested or even actively critical. Not everyone has practiced presenting sufficiently to be able to discern some of these subtle states of connection or disconnection, but tellers should be generally aware of the relationship between audience and story.

Between teller and audience is a relationship that rests on trust. At a minimum, the audience trusts that the teller is saying something worth hearing, which makes them willing to listen. An audience's trust in the storyteller is the foundation of successful leadership and motivational or persuasive storytelling. Audiences willing to be persuaded are willing to trust the storyteller. A deep form of this kind of trust underpins spiritual or religious stories about why we are here and the meaning of our existence. Library data stories are generally less deep than this but are very meaningful in their own way, as they support the longevity and health of informed communities that form the basis of a democratic society. The relationship between teller and audience can be so powerful that it is dangerous, as when political leaders exploit their power as storytellers to manipulate groups. Library data storytellers should be aware of this relationship but should emphasize story first. The humble attitude of the teller in service to the story not only forms the heart of the LIS storytelling tradition, but it also sustains a healthy relationship between teller and audience.

How Familiarity Influences the Relationship Between Teller and Audience

The relationship between teller and audience depends on how familiar the audience is with the teller and each other. In storytelling of any kind, how the audience views the teller is based on how well they are (or are not) acquainted with the teller. Table 4.1 explores the four possibilities of familiarity between teller and audience.

These four possibilities will vary depending on degrees of familiarity, the proportion of the audience that is familiar or not familiar with the teller, and more. Considering these questions provides basic guidelines for any data storyteller who is navigating a relationship with an audience.

Revisiting Cultural Competence

While equitable relationships between teller and audience and among audience members are best, the reality is more complex. Each person inhabits a variety of cultural spaces and identities that intersect with one another, and we each exist at the edge of some and in the center of others. These cultures and identities can be visible or invisible and can be perceived or imposed on people without their consent, such as misgendering or other forms of othering. Cultures and identities can also be embraced and expressed willingly, such as when people share their relationship to a story.

As discussed in chapter 1, in storytelling, cultural competence respects how the audience's lived experiences, cultures, and positionalities differ from the

TABLE 4.1
Four Familiarity Possibilities Between Teller and Audience

	AUDIENCE MEMBERS FAMILIAR WITH EACH OTHER	AUDIENCE MEMBERS UNFAMILIAR WITH EACH OTHER
Familiar Teller	How can the teller prime the audience to hear unexpected messages? How can the teller surprise them while also sustaining trust?	How can the teller help them connect to the information in this story, despite familiarity? How does laughter or other collective reaction indicate connection?
Unfamiliar Teller	How can the teller acknowledge their prior connection? How can the teller draw on or encourage their collegiality?	How can the teller deliver what was advertised? How can the teller respond appropriately to unexpected dynamics?

teller's. There are infinite variations of how people are (and are perceived) culturally (e.g., racially, ethnically, linguistically, and more). Audiences will not share exactly the same cultural identities as the teller. Even when they do share most of the same identities, individual people will be at the center of some cultural identities while those same people may be at the margin of other identities. Imagine a library director who is also a biracial single parent: a professional event will center their role as a leader; at a family reunion, their cultural and parenting identities are central; as a mentor to BIPOC staff and interns, their racial identity and lived experience of racism may be an important common ground; and in any context, racial microaggressions may force the individual's biracial identity into the center of a moment, sometimes violently and without their consent. Whether this hypothetical person's experiences reflect some, all, or none of your experiences, cultural competence means respecting that this person's lived experiences, cultures, and positionalities bring that person to a place of knowledge of all their identities.

Cultural humility means striving for equitable and just relationships while understanding that there are power imbalances in interactions, including the reality that the storyteller has a position of power in relation to the audience, and so must practice critical self-reflection (Hurley et al. 2022). It would be challenging, if not impossible, to map all the possible relationships between teller and audience. Still, issues like culture, identity, and familiarity are key factors that deserve particular attention when considering how tellers express themselves alongside their stories and how audiences may tend to listen (or not). Understanding the possible combinations of simpler concepts like familiarity/ unfamiliarity can provide a set of questions that may also be useful for considering the deeper complexities related to culture, identity, and more.

With these richer understandings of the storytelling triangle, we can turn to three key ways a teller can know and understand audiences: knowledge, demographics, and attitudes.

Audience Knowledge

Audiences come to library data stories with preexisting understandings and experiences. What they know matters, especially about library data. This *knowledge* matters not only for how audiences understand library data stories, but also what they think libraries should become in the future and how they will vote—as elected representatives or as citizens—to fund or defund library initiatives and services. This section focuses on audiences whose knowledge levels will impact the outcomes for libraries, from the administrators in organizations to the boards that oversee libraries or their governing educational institutions. The knowledge of these groups has two components, *context* and *data*, and we must consider not only what they know but also strategies for assessing their knowledge.

Audience Knowledge of Library Context

Years ago, in one of my PhD courses, I was speaking with information science students who asked me, "Why don't people just buy their own books?" At that moment, I understood that these students came from affluent backgrounds and had no experience of being unable to buy anything that they wanted to read, watch, or play. In this context, understanding people's knowledge of libraries may also mean revealing something about how their own privilege has kept them from knowing the value of libraries. Just as white privilege can create ignorance of racism, economic privilege can result in ignorance about the benefits of libraries.

Some people serving on the governing boards of libraries are deeply familiar with the library context and are perhaps even former librarians themselves. Others will have professional backgrounds with parallel ethics regarding privacy, such as health care workers and medical records, so that library privacy practices are easy to translate for them. For others, these ideals and what they mean in practice may be new. The next two subsections offer a primer on the basic functions of libraries and the concept of intellectual freedom.

Library Basics

What are libraries? At the most basic level, libraries are community resources that exist to benefit everyone. They are especially important for those who cannot afford to buy access to books and other media. Knowing this context involves understanding the library itself as an institution, its everyday practices, and the reasons behind those practices, which in turn includes understanding the professional ethics that inform libraries' choices, including what they do and do not routinely collect as data. For example, libraries regularly collect numbers representing circulation, registered library cardholders, the people and households in communities, foot traffic, public computer use, website access, database access, and much more. Because of their longstanding ethical commitment to readers' privacy, however, library systems do not perpetually store the names of people who borrowed specific books or accessed certain resources. Or, if the systems do store this information, libraries do not share this information beyond the need for circulation records.

Intellectual Freedom Basics

Understanding libraries requires understanding the basic principles of intellectual freedom. Intellectual freedom is "the right of library users to read, seek information, and speak freely as guaranteed by the First Amendment" (ALA 2018). The "freedom to read" is a broad concept in a diverse society, and it encompasses both positive rights (e.g., the freedom to access and to receive information) and negative rights (e.g., the freedom from privacy invasion) (ALA 2006).

It is clearer than ever that libraries have an ongoing role in educating the public about the ideals of intellectual freedom. This work, however, may be challenging when governing board members misunderstand intellectual freedom or bring their own competing ideologies to the table of decision-makers.

Assessing Your Library's Governance

Knowledge of a library's context is always as multidimensional and complex as the learning experiences of each person. Finding out what board members, for example, and other stakeholders who govern funding know about libraries as organizations can be challenging. When new board members are appointed, unless they are publicly known to hold specific ideologies, it may be difficult to assess their knowledge about libraries. Conversations about knowledge are easiest to have individually, starting with questions like, "So what made you interested in being appointed to the library board?" When individual conversations are impossible, as with the boards of trustees of large educational institutions, then internet research is often the only option. Understanding the professional backgrounds of people in these roles, while not a comprehensive indicator of their knowledge, offers a sense of how they are likely to approach problem-solving or understand library goals. For example, some board members will bring a knowledge of technology or business that is informed primarily by engineering or marketing perspectives, perhaps with a vision of people as resources for data mining.

You may also assess your library board's knowledge by asking simple questions about their experiences. Requesting a show of hands or a quick recap about what they know can provide a wealth of information. Consider questions like:

- Who here participated in the last library survey of the community, as a community member?
- Who here remembers seeing the last library presentation about circulation data?
- How many of you have been part of the development of a library budget presentation before?
- Who here was on the board the last time we started a strategic planning process?

Frame these questions positively, seeking those with likely positive answers. Try to identify those who have knowledge rather than accidentally exposing and embarrassing those who do not. You can ask similar questions that probe board members' experience with surveys, budgets, or strategic planning in related work for other organizations, whether in professional roles or on other boards.

Assessing Your Library Staff

Knowledge of context also varies among the people working in the library. The size of a library usually determines the extent of the division of labor and specialization. In very small libraries, one or just a handful of people play all the roles. In very large library systems, there may be multiple data experts and multiple directors who have responsibilities for communicating the purposes of libraries at the level of systems, branches, programs, and more. Data can be lost in translation between the groups inside libraries. For example, communications and public relations staff may not speak the same language as front-line library staff who deal with the public. Sometimes those responsible for making periodic reports to governing agencies, ranging from budget requests to state-level library data reporting, can be very isolated if the staff and governing boards do not have a solid knowledge of library data. You should consider training in data literacy for all members of the staff.

Audience Knowledge of Library Data

Decision-makers and anyone other than library experts rarely have a deep knowledge of library data. So, from the start, the assumption must be that most decision-making audiences need presentations of and about library data that will let them learn quickly and easily. That said, some decision-makers will have a knowledge of data from some other context, whether professional or nonprofit, which can translate reasonably well into the library context. Especially when comparing relatively simple data that describes quantifiable things—like the numbers of programs, loans, or cardholders from year to year—the practices from other professions can provide similar points of view.

See table 4.2 to consider how a few common types of library data might be similar or even analogous to the data in other settings.

Many types of data will be familiar to audiences. Automated systems reports exist in most business and nonprofit settings, and many audiences will be familiar with quarterly reports that assess progress toward yearly goals, rates of budget expenditure, and other metrics. Counting library interactions with people (e.g., library cards/registered borrowers, program attendance, public computer use, visitors) will be familiar to any public-facing nonprofit or business that serves large numbers of clients. Data about service hours and website visits can help determine when and how to provide ways of connecting to library patrons. Libraries' service hours relate to usage patterns that will be especially familiar to local or regional businesses that have brick-and-mortar locations. Website visits will be familiar to any organization with a significant online presence that allows users to access its resources online.

TABLE 4.2
Some Types of Library Data and Similar Business Data

LIBRARY DATA	SIMILAR BUSINESS DATA
Automated systems reports, such as financial transactions	Cash flow statements
Library cards/registered borrowers	Client counts
Program attendance	Webinar registration
Public computer use	Online assessment participation
Visitors	Foot traffic counts
Service hours	Hours of operation
Website visits	Website visits

Some data practices, however, do not translate very well and may feel unfamiliar to audiences. For example, libraries are anchored to communities, whether geographically through taxing districts or institutionally through educational organizations. From a twenty-first-century business standpoint, only a few sectors, such as construction, infrastructure maintenance, and local or regional development, are entirely geographically anchored. To give another example, libraries exist in dialogue with their communities, which do not just consume their resources but share in the public stewardship of the library in a way that is quite distinct from a customer's relationship to a business. Similarly, business practices based on statistical inferences, including attempted market forecasting, can be more controversial because libraries must respond to unpredictable demographic shifts. A typical business may assume that market analysis will identify its target audience with relative stability, but a library's target audience may grow, shrink, or shift demographically over time. While concepts of organizational agility apply across contexts, especially since the 2020 global pandemic, how a teller frames agility for an audience differs greatly from business perspectives that view people as potential customers. Library perspectives may use the word *customer* too, but libraries fundamentally view people as those to be served (Gorman 2000).

Determining the Audience's Data Literacy

Library board members and administrators with experience in data analytics, however, can be assets to the decision-making processes. In many cases, knowing how to look at data to find interesting correlations is a transferable skill. Associating data about people with data about library practices or community needs can be a unifying exercise, especially for library boards. Table 4.3 revisits the three audience types from chapter 3 (general public, executives, and professionals) to show how to assess their general data literacy by asking open-ended questions.

Facilitating Data Best Practices for Audiences

Some people may feel pressured to appear to understand data even if they do not have any background in it. Many audience members are not educated in data analysis best practices. This can lead people to bad data practices like cherry-picking data unknowingly. The best data storytelling comes from collaborative work between data experts, storytellers, and carefully selected rehearsal audiences. Larger libraries will have data experts, while smaller libraries may

TABLE 4.3
Determining Audience Data Literacy

AUDIENCE TYPE	REQUIREMENTS	QUERIES TO DETERMINE AUDIENCE DATA LITERACY
General Public	Understand data	What would you like to know about the library?
Executives	High-level overview of data trends to aid strategic decision-making	What information can library data provide to help you make decisions?
Professionals	Detailed insights to understand the phenomenon behind data	What types of data do you need to understand the current impact of the library?

need to cultivate knowledgeable board members or colleagues as allies to help with presentations to governing boards.

To facilitate such collaborations, the data and its interpretation should be as clear as possible, especially if an intended audience includes people who do not really understand the basics of library data. You should strive to:

- Show as much as possible. Translate data into visuals, and reinforce the most important meanings with images, words, and other annotations.
- Caption the images. Doing so is best accessibility practice, but it also forces a final translation back from visuals to phrases that can frame a story.
- Share data visualizations with practice audiences and ask what they think the main takeaways are. Improve the visualizations based on this feedback.

Overall, knowing as much as possible about the knowledge of the audience is a solid starting point for effective data storytelling, especially when the audience has the power to make decisions that affect the future of the library. Audiences who include the general public require a broader lens, with a focus on demographics.

Audience Demographics

Serving a large and diverse public is an immense privilege, one that comes with the challenge of how to know your audience. Audience *demographics* are another tool that can provide parts of the picture. Demographic data useful to libraries may come from the library's own records, the community, or from comparisons or contrasts with other libraries.

Types of Demographic Data

There are many types of demographic data. The list below provides examples of some types of data that are most pertinent to library data storytelling.

- Overall number of constituents, whether patrons or students
- Languages spoken in households in the library community
- Household income levels in the library community
- Neighborhoods or other geographic factors, such as colleges within a university
- Ages or age ranges of community members
- Community members' cultural groups with which people actively affiliate, whether ethnic, religious, social, or something else
- Community members' work roles and positions, including sectors and industries where people are employed

Demographics can be powerful in providing a very general picture of audience interests and elements of identity. They are limited, however, and should be used thoughtfully and cautiously when attempting to infer people's interests. For example, while many federal records will include race, racial categories in the US census have a troubled history (Wilkerson 2020). Without having lived or learned this history, it is far too easy to replicate and amplify discriminatory stereotypes. Using demographic data requires a commitment to education and cultural competence about demographic categories.

Demographics, Discrimination, and Poverty

Despite the potential for harmful misuse, demographic data is vital to understanding audiences. For example, libraries have a responsibility to make information accessible in the languages that people speak in their communities. Knowing what languages other than English are spoken will provide libraries with a direct way to assess their collections and improve information access. Further investigating what languages people in the community speak who have lower household income levels adds a rationale for bolstering and advertising language-accessible collections.

Poverty, however, carries stigma. Arguments based on household income should be made carefully and emphasize people's humanity. The first important consideration is to not exploit people by using their stories of trauma to justify library ends. Although there may be stark inequities in income, education, and more, characterizing groups of people solely in terms of deficits is not only unkind but can amplify harm. The second consideration is to look at the effect on the audience of difficult stories. Sometimes they need to hear them, but at other times those stories can have a disconnecting effect because of the level of emotion involved—more on this later. Decision-making audiences can easily be overwhelmed by emotionally fraught stories of suffering. While some audience members will want to know more, others will go numb and tune out, falling back upon stereotypes they learned from an implicitly biased culture and leading to further dehumanization.

There is rarely a need, then, to tell another person's story of trauma in order to justify the work of the library. When representing trauma for library purposes, it is usually best practice for library workers to frame their arguments in terms of statistical information like income levels, rather than individual stories of impoverishment that could expose people to additional suffering through reputational harm. The data does not always require a human story if that story would negatively characterize a person or group. Retelling stories of suffering tends to dehumanize, turning people into statistics or mere representatives of disaster rather than whole human beings. A rich and trusting relationship between libraries and communities will create room for people to tell their own stories, when and if they choose to do so—as discussed in chapter 2.

At the same time, if the audience is challenged to understand the situation that people in poverty face, it can be helpful to walk through everyday life scenarios. Consider data that represents concrete issues like the time necessary to travel to two or three jobs, the sleeping hours available to those who work two or more jobs, and the time available to support children with homework help. Consider representing typical household budget expenses in light of the local cost of living and median wages. Show the challenges in statistical terms that represent real people without affording the audience an opportunity to activate their own implicit biases. Insist that the audience see people facing poverty as people striving to overcome obstacles. In this light, the availability of a library and its resources become a more vivid contribution to community life, education, and wellness.

Assumptions about people based on demographics can sometimes backfire, so drawing inferences based on demographics can only be a starting point. For example, a recent ALA report indicates trends among younger adults who value the library and prefer to use print collections (Berens and Noorda 2023). These preferences contradict the assumption that so-called "digital native" generations prefer e-books. In other words, keeping up with demographic research can counter commonly held assumptions and anchor library practices in relevant data. Repeating stories that reinforce false or negative stereotypes about groups of people harms communities and the libraries that serve them.

Demographics and Context

Demographics are always contextual, and it is important to consider the factors that might impact cultural groups and their relationship to libraries. In addition to the spoken languages represented in library collections, these factors might include the languages and cultures represented in programs, library locations in relation to neighborhood populations, and transit options to the library. Frankly, it is likely that a marginalized cultural group will have already experienced negative stereotypes from mainstream groups—possibly including library workers. Library workers must not, through their own ignorance or lack of preparation, further contribute to that harm. We should never assume that demographic data stands in for attitudes or viewpoints.

We should instead focus on the assets that a cultural group brings to the library. For example, at a recent talk, an award-winning library director described her practice, as a Latinx leader, of going to schools, parks, and even grocery stores where people share her culture, and challenging them to find out more about the library. Her strategy, known as "targeted community engagement," worked. The library saw massive increases in foot traffic, program attendance, website use, and more. Now she has moved on to another predominantly Latinx community where she expects to be able to make the same types of changes (Research Institute for Public Libraries 2023).

Overall, focusing on libraries' opportunities to serve their communities means drawing from demographic data with careful professional judgment. See box 4.1 for more on how to work through bias, respect the audience, and build trust.

> **BOX 4.1**
> *Reflection and Respecting the Audience*
>
> Respecting the audience builds trust and enables our stories to be heard and retold. Respect for the audience is not an abstract concept, and in some cases, it may not be simple. As discussed earlier, storytelling occurs in the same social and cultural spaces where bias, discrimination, and systemic injustices are part of the fabric of everyday life. This means that storytellers face different biases the moment they take the stage, depending on their audience members' preconceptions and the work they have (or have not) done to grow beyond stereotyped ways of thinking about people. At the same time, because the storyteller wants the audience to hear them, they must do their own work to internally reflect on, unpack, and mitigate their own biases. Depending on the outcome, the teller will be either more or less capable of respecting the audience.

Audience Attitudes

Audiences have *attitudes* that vary widely, whether among the different individuals in an audience or even within the individual audience members themselves over time. Attitudes derive from circumstances that, taken as a whole, are as complex as the world we inhabit. Commonalities when it comes to storytelling to different audiences, however, can help prepare the data storyteller to connect with different attitudes and know where to put their energy.

Knowing Your Audience's Attitude

In advocacy contexts or any communication of impact to stakeholders, it is valuable to know how the audience thinks about any specific story, proposal, or topic. Audience attitudes can be established in conversations with individual members of a board of trustees, for example, by floating an idea, or by examining the history of their reactions to similar ideas. The democratic nature of these deliberations means that it is vital to acknowledge that people have the right to disagree. It may be impossible to know exactly what all the attitudes are in a particular audience, and there are circumstances in which audiences change as well, in terms of both their composition and their attitudes.

A key audience, in the case of libraries, consists of the stakeholders who have a vote. Much of library governance hinges on people reaching a decision based on a vote. My guidance about audiences is based on my own experiences as a leader, as a storytelling consultant to many nonprofit organizations, and as a library board member. The insights offered here, however, are based on research interviews held with more than 100 information professionals in libraries and related fields, and have been expanded and validated through qualitative research with a team of 40 librarians. This section provides some guidance for managing audiences who have different attitudes about shared realities, and for mitigating the struggles of trying to communicate with audiences who do not share a common reality. Because of the different strategies required, the first four types of audiences—positive, negative, mixed, and indifferent—are grouped together, while the fifth—polarized—has a separate section.

Positive, Negative, Mixed, and Indifferent Audiences

Positive, negative, mixed, and indifferent audiences have attitudes based on their differing interpretations of the same reality, situation, or data. They might agree, for instance, that refreshing a computer lab would help the library provide better service, but they would disagree about whether that expense is worth it. A positive audience would agree that the expense is worth it. A negative audience would think that the expense is not worth it, or that there are other issues that are of higher priority. A mixed audience would combine some of both of these attitudes.

Positive audiences are the easiest to work with because they are already favorably inclined toward the argument of a data story. The teller's tone can be open with these audiences, and the communication tactics will be about building and sustaining trust. Positive audiences are poised to retell the story, so the teller must give them a good story to tell. They will want to understand the data so that, like all stakeholders, they can explain to others why they voted the way they did. They need a clear argument with evidence, and a story they can tell about why they support that argument, so the teller should repeat their message to reinforce its value. Members of positive audiences, however, can change their views, so tellers should avoid overestimating their sympathy. No one likes to be taken for granted, and tellers should expect even positive audiences to bring some clarifying questions to the discussion.

Negative audiences are difficult but not impossible to work with because they may be possible to persuade. The first tactic is to stay on message and not take any negativity personally, maintaining a calm tone in the face of opposition. The goal is to find a point of agreement and build a proposal together with the audience, hoping to persuade or to locate some common ground upon which to reach agreement. While a negative audience may dismiss or even undermine the teller or the story, remember that such aggressive behavior may be hiding the concern, reluctance, or even fear they feel. If people express these feelings, the teller might turn these into common ideas for modifying the proposal. The teller can also slow down their own responses in order to de-escalate a negative audience's reaction. By listening patiently, acknowledging audience members' concerns, and restating them in positive terms, a teller may be able to persuade a negative audience. Even if they are not persuaded, it may still be possible to compromise and make some progress by preparing differently for next time.

Mixed audiences are very common and consist of some people with positive attitudes about the story and some with negative ones. With such audiences, the teller's tone should be both open and calm, maintaining professional distance in the face of negative comments. The best practice is to tell a coherent data story designed to persuade, but to first craft that story using the input of rehearsal audiences. If negative audience members are persuaded, subsequently they will need a great story to explain why they changed their minds. Respect for audiences means that the teller does not tell someone else what their story should be, but instead considers that the person will need a good reason for going along with something that they initially opposed. If clear data underpins the reason, and that data is easy to retell as a story, then negative audience members will be more likely to change their minds. Additionally, a compelling story may inspire positive audience members to persuade negative audience members.

Indifferent audiences are more likely to be part of the general public and less likely to be part of a voting body that will make decisions. Indifference itself has many causes. In data storytelling, the most likely cause is that the audience does not see how data in general or the specific data being communicated relates to what they care about. In this case, data is really the source of patterns that represent experiences, ideas, or people that an indifferent audience might be persuaded to care about. To connect with this audience, the teller should start with why the story matters and be specific about how the library or the relevant data is already affecting their lives. Even if the audience does not respond, it is important for the teller to remain engaged and model the interest that they hope to instill. Keep the message very simple for an indifferent audience as a means of engaging their interest. Finally, ask questions and wait through an awkward pause for responses. This kind of interaction might feel uncomfortable, but it is a normal part of attempting to engage an indifferent audience.

Sometimes audiences are indifferent because they are numb. Data can cause people to simply disengage. Deeply troubling psychological research finds that, when faced with large amounts of data—such as deaths during the COVID-19 pandemic and its aftermath—people simply tune out. Research on the representation of large groups indicates that, when faced with massive amounts of wrongdoing, people become overwhelmed and do nothing. For example, in cases of mass murder and genocide, reports of large "numbers of deaths fail to spark emotion or feeling and thus fail to motivate action" (Slovic 2007, 79). Although libraries rarely need to recount stories of suffering, it is worth noting that while such stories may motivate others to act, these moral impulses often falter or fade away at a large scale.

In terms of data, people routinely feel overwhelmed and powerless when faced with large-scale errors or injustices, which are even more devastating when part of a pattern of systematic discouragement or disenfranchisement by social systems designed to create obstacles between people and their right to social support. Such was the case in Indiana with the automation of benefit programs that left certain children without medical benefits, denying them and their families "benefits, due process, dignity, and life itself" (Eubanks 2018, 83).

Similarly, in spring 2023, about 250,000 people received letters from the Florida state government stating that they were no longer eligible for Medicaid. Some received letters saying they might be eligible for a different kind of access to Medicaid if they reapplied, but the reapplication paperwork was complex and confusing, and people, including my own brother did not know where to turn. Our whole family read and reread the information, struggling to understand the financial implications of the additional out-of-pocket cost of $700 per month if my brother—as a person with multiple disabilities—could no longer afford his medical bills. Of the 250,000 people who were dropped and told to reapply, 82 percent of them were misinformed; they were actually still eligible to receive benefits (Pederson 2023). As of fall 2023, 120,000 children in Florida had been denied Medicaid (O'Donnell 2023). As of summer 2020, at least 1.8 million Floridians had been removed from Medicaid, and some allege inadequate opportunity to address the basis of the removal (Blake 2024). Lawsuits are ongoing. The fear aroused by these huge numbers of people whose lives are threatened is real, and it is reasonable for audiences hearing these stories to feel overwhelmed and thus become numb and indifferent to the data and information.

Overall, tellers must remember that behind some seemingly indifferent audiences are people who are simply overwhelmed. If the teller can reach these audiences with a data story about what libraries can offer to communities, then these people might engage with the data and turn to libraries for help. Based on the above example, a library staff member helping someone complete a Medicaid reapplication form on a library computer could potentially save a family about $700 per month in out-of-pocket costs. This story shows the tangible and immediate financial benefits of a carefully told data story and a helpful library staff member in the face of overwhelming governmental errors.

Polarized Audiences

Polarized audiences are becoming more common, not just in the United States but around the globe. Recent decades have witnessed the rise of authoritarian leaders who expect obedience to their story without question (Diamond et al. 2016), and this trend has sparked renewed historical interest in twentieth-century totalitarian movements (Snyder 2017). Most democratic leaders expect to be able to establish a shared truth across different belief systems for the public good. In contrast, authoritarian leaders expect obedience to their worldview, even when it is false. Leaders who encourage violence against those who resist them create polarized audiences. For example, the January 6, 2021, attack on the US Capitol demonstrates how a democratically elected president who had lost his reelection bid attempted to overthrow the legitimate election results based on the false story that the election had been "stolen" (Starbird et al. 2023).

Polarized audiences consist of people who hold wildly divergent points of view about, for instance, what a public institution is for, or whether there should be public institutions at all. Some people in these audiences come with a shared reality (whether positive, negative, or mixed) and can agree to a common understanding of what the data shows, even if they disagree about what to do based on that data. Polarized audiences, however, also consist of people who spread false information, and it is crucial for tellers not to repeat or amplify false information in the process of trying to address it. Repetition reinforces, and audience members are more likely to remember something that is repeated, even if it is false, than they are to remember a more nuanced truth or compromise.

The first step in approaching a polarized audience is to *identify the problem.* One way is to notice whether certain audience members consistently deflect from a commonly grounded understanding of the data and instead bring up controversies that are not directly related to the data. Another indicator might be that attempts to discuss interpretations of data quickly turn into veiled or direct accusations about who is wrong or immoral. A third indication of a problem might be when limits are placed on conversations about equity or inequity, so that asking questions about inequities or unfair treatment is discouraged or even becomes illegal, thus damaging communities' ability to see social divides clearly and accurately. Each of these is an example of a larger pattern of dividing people against each other, using debate to shut down those who disagree rather than coming to a shared agreement. If the conversation consistently returns to who is wrong or bad while avoiding the actual topic, then this may be a polarized audience.

The second step in managing storytelling to a polarized audience is *determining what to do about the problem.* If stakeholders are deeply divided in their understanding of reality, or if a majority are invested in authoritarian obedience, then the situation is very dire. Recent appointments to the higher education board of trustees in Florida demonstrate how authoritarian leaders can create polarized audiences. At the small liberal arts New College of Florida, the librarian was fired without warning and eligible faculty members were denied promotion (Moody 2024). Stacking the state board of education with people who want to transform public universities into Christian colleges leaves no room for a shared understanding of public higher education; people either agree or disagree that public institutions should be Christian. The Florida governor used extraordinary measures by adding many seats to the board, including out-of-state Twitter (X) celebrities, to artificially create a majority who share his bias that non-Christians do not belong. This shift toward a Christian affiliation contradicts the constitutional separation of church and state in the United States. Given the complete revamping by the governor, those with power remain unchecked in continuing to dehumanize the faculty and staff of the New College of Florida to impose their exclusionary worldview.

In many cases, however, the situation is not this dire. There are many library boards and school boards with just a handful of members who hold views opposing the possibility of a shared understanding of reality. Identifying these views can be tricky, but they usually consist of arguments that certain people or groups of people are wrong or evil. Another way to identify these views is by looking at the storytelling dynamics. If there seems to be only one possible way to interpret a story, and if there is no way to disagree without seeming to be a bad person, then the audience is polarized.

The third step in approaching storytelling to a polarized audience is to *determine when to persuade and when to avoid debate.* Because attempts to persuade open the door to debate, the teller should consider the value of debate strategically. When a small group of misinformed people are actively spreading misinformation to others, they may deliberately use an opening for debate to confuse the issues at hand. For example, the white supremacist Steve Bannon calls his followers to "flood the zone," meaning they should create confusion and chaos rather than engage in earnest debate. Bannon was the chief White House strategist during the first Trump administration who went to prison for refusing to cooperate with the courts (Khalil 2022). Connecting the Bannon example to library data storytelling, if the teller identifies someone in a polarized audience who mocks the decision-making process, uses debate to create confusion, or dehumanizes certain people or groups, that person may be trying to "flood the zone" with bad information because confusion allows them to more easily take power (Stelter 2021; Ulusoy et al. 2021).

The fourth step in approaching storytelling to a polarized audience when the teller is trying to manage misinformation is to *stay on message.* Repeating the same message even while being goaded to debate may seem hostile, but if done with a calm tone, it can be a peaceful tactic to preserve the possibility of decision-making. In addition to staying on message with a polarized audience, the teller should avoid distractions and not repeat false information in an attempt to refute it. Ultimately, the teller's goal with a polarized audience is to win over the majority of the voting stakeholders and minimize distractions.

To summarize, each type of audience attitude requires the teller to adopt a slightly different tone and tactics to ensure that the data is heard, the message remains clear, and the story can be as persuasive as possible. Table 4.4 provides a quick overview of the various strategies as they relate to audience attitudes.

Conclusion: Critical Listening

Many data stories are told effectively, yet they do not result in change. Why would a well-documented story about social inequities in a community not result in change? One explanation of this considers audience reactions that dismiss or even do not hear the story in the first place. For example, if an audience is so

TABLE 4.4
Quick Guide to Audience Attitudes

ATTITUDE	SHARED REALITY?	TONE	TACTICS
Positive	Yes	Open	Build trust. Don't take audience sympathy for granted. Make the story easy to retell.
Negative	Yes	Calm	Focus on persuasion. Restate concerns in positive terms to build common ground. Find compromises, even if disagreements continue. Slow down to de-escalate conflict.
Mixed	Yes	Open and calm	If some are persuaded, consider the story they need to tell about why.
Indifferent	Yes	Curious	Start with why it matters for these specific people. Model the interest that you hope to instill. Keep it simple. Ask questions and wait for responses.
Polarized	No	Non-reactive	Stay on message. Do not repeat false information. Consider the value of debate strategically. If the intent is to confuse the voters, avoid debate.

unfamiliar with a perspective that it seems intuitively wrong to them, then some audience members may contradict or even deliberately overpower the voices of those with different experiences. As library advocates it is crucial to be prepared for such dynamics.

Considering the Context of a Story

To be effective library data storytellers and advocates, we must unpack the implications of an audience's preexisting beliefs, bias, and numbness. First, we must understand the *context* of the story. Audiences live, work, and learn in contexts, and if those contexts have embedded patterns that will make some data more difficult to communicate, the teller must attempt to know that in advance. Consider a community where there has been prior reluctance to defend intellectual freedom in libraries. Ignoring that context is likely to lead such a community to dismiss any data story about the right to read because it contradicts the status quo narrative; namely, that some books should be banned and libraries are complacent or even sinister in providing "dangerous" books for children. However, it would be a disservice to the community to accept the terms of this debate at face value. It is necessary to assert the importance of access to information and the ways that libraries support families across the community who have many different backgrounds and perspectives.

An audience's understanding, or lack thereof, of a particular context will impact their ability to listen. For example, racism and sexism frequently remain invisible to an organization's members, both to the "insiders" who benefit from its affordances and to the "outsiders" who may become numb over time because of systematic othering. For insiders, the teller-audience relationship locks into certain narratives and ignores others. Outsiders may be necessary to reveal the normalized, invisible racism and sexism. As one person shared with me in a private conversation, their higher education institution has some problems with inequity, and especially sexual harassment, gender harassment, gender inequality, and racial inequality, like many other institutions. However, when these problems came up in an external review, she acknowledged that it was possible that the leadership did not realize this was an issue. Knowing a context does not necessarily mean practicing consistent and critical listening to understand people's perspectives in that context (see box 4.2).

BOX 4.2
Whose Story Is It?

Concerning institutional or organizational stories, the teller should consider the ethics of sharing and re-sharing personal and cultural stories. Considering to whom an institutional story belongs requires remembering that institutions are made up of people of different cultures. The cases below offer best practices for cultural competence and library data storytelling about people, cultures, and institutions.

- *People* have stories, and those stories are best shared by them directly.
    - Stories about personal suffering should only be shared by the individual, not retold by others.
    - If sharing a story about a person would cause them any kind of harm—psychological, social, economic, reputational—then *do not* retell or ask to retell that story.
    - If a person's story does not require identifying information, then, just as in qualitative research standards, the story should be anonymized.
    - If anonymization is impossible and a version of the story can be amalgamated from multiple people's experiences, then the story should be created as a hypothetical experience with accurate representation of a trend or pattern.
    - If a person's story is to be ethically re-shared to support a library, then the person should be fully informed about the time, place, teller, and intention of retelling, and their consent to this use and retelling of their story should be obtained.

- *Cultures* have stories, and people have complex relationships to cultures.
    - A person's position in relation to a culture should determine whether a cultural story is theirs to tell. People are insiders and outsiders, at the center of some and on the margins of other cultures. Understanding someone's positionality requires both skillful reflection and judgment.

(continued on p. 108)

Box 4.2 (continued)

- Cultures are difficult for outsiders to understand. If a story represents a culture to which the teller does not belong, consider inviting someone more appropriate to be the storyteller.
- If there are cross-cultural educational or communication reasons for telling a story of a culture to which you do not belong, then approach the storytelling with humility. When receiving critical feedback, especially if someone says, "I'm from this culture and you're not telling the story right," thank them for the feedback and ask for more information.
- If someone from a culture tells you that you should not tell a story, then do not tell it.

- *Institutions* have stories and cultures.
  - Institutions have people who belong to them in the present, as well as long histories of stewardship by others from the past.
  - An institution's stories should cause no harm to people or to the institutional culture.
  - Leaders must often tell institutional stories. Those stories should be iteratively developed with rehearsal audiences who represent as many groups as possible within the institution.

In addition to these cases, knowing who owns a story may be unclear, contested, or even deliberately confusing. Libraries as institutions have a responsibility to communicate with the people whose community supports the library, those who work at the library, and those who are disconnected from the library but could benefit from its resources. Telling a powerful institutional story requires consideration and thoughtfulness, but it is a key way to connect the work of the library with the community and support library data advocacy.

Considering the Preexisting Bias of an Audience

Second, just as we must consider context in storytelling, so must we consider the possible *preexisting bias* of an audience. Stories go unheard when they come up against existing biases. Biased patterns of beliefs are both individual and social. They are sustained and easily amplified by groups, consciously or unconsciously. Human defensiveness stemming from unconscious biases can lead stories to be rejected—even the most data-rich and well-evidenced stories—if they do not fit prior beliefs. For example, telling stories of women's suffering from domestic violence and wage inequities has not always won women equality. As Francesca Polletta's (2006) detailed sociological analysis of narrative in social movements indicates, women who defend themselves against criminal charges in domestic violence cases are sometimes seen as "strong-willed and unapologetic; not a proper victim but someone using her abuse to get herself off the hook." Similarly, in cases of wage inequity, when a woman aspires to the same jobs and pay as men, "she is heard as claiming there are no differences between men and women" (140).

Recently, an elected leader who advocates for unhoused people privately shared a story with me about requesting that a water fountain be installed in a downtown plaza. They asked for this change so that dogs and babies/nursing mothers could easily access water, but unhoused people would also benefit. This individual told me, "But they [city officials] won't do it for 'homeless people.' Everybody wants dogs and babies to have water, but not 'the homeless.'" Both versions of this story are true. Dogs, babies, and people would all benefit from the new water fountain. Which version of the story is told depends on the audience and their biases. Though it is desirable to change hearts and minds, when advocating for specific resources, it is not always necessary to challenge the audience's biases. If a subset of true stories achieves the desired result, choose a true story that resonates most with the audience.

Considering Different Interpretations of a Narrative

Finally, being prepared for a different *interpretation* of a narrative and making the public's values—not those of the librarians—clear and compelling will raise the probability that a different narrative will be more persuasive. If there must be a debate over intellectual freedom, then it should be accompanied by individual stories of those stakeholders whose lives have been changed by reading. Why would a reader need a book? Who needs that book? What does it mean to read broadly and in ways that reflect all kinds of lives, perspectives, and societies? In this kind of context, stories about the benefits of reading will be more powerful if they are backed by both evidence from data and stories of readers' lived experiences.

The goal of critical data storytelling is to persuade honestly with data, but contending with the audience's understanding of context requires consideration, thoughtfulness, and honest grappling with how people receive or ignore stories depending on their experiences or lack thereof. And because data stories may either confirm or disrupt preexisting beliefs and biases, library advocates must also grapple with the complexities of fake news, false data, and misinformation, as we will explore in chapter 5.

FURTHER READINGS

Del Negro, Janice M. 2017. *Engaging Teens with Story: How to Inspire and Educate Youth with Storytelling.* Libraries Unlimited.
> Teenagers and resistant library board members may be among the more difficult audiences in the world. This guide to storytelling for teen audiences presents classic narratives that connect with this life phase.

Lipman, Doug. 1999. *Improving Your Storytelling: Beyond the Basics for All Who Tell Stories in Work or Play.* August House.
> The author is a nationally recognized storytelling coach, and his book is a classic for reflecting on one's own abilities and limitations as a storytelling performer, with guidance on how to grow through difficult storytelling situations.

Niemi, Loren, and Elizabeth Ellis. 2001. *Inviting the Wolf In: Thinking About the Difficult Story.* August House.
> A difficult story is any story whose content makes it challenging to tell or difficult to hear. Although these authors focus on emotionally difficult content rather than social injustices, stories related to long-term injustices and current crises of politics and trust will be improved by attending to emotional content in some of the ways they describe.

REFERENCES

ALA American Library Association. 2006. "Library Bill of Rights." Advocacy, Legislation & Issues. www.ala.org/advocacy/intfreedom/librarybill.

ALA. 2018. "Support for Intellectual Freedom." Tools, Publications & Resources. www.ala.org/tools/challengesupport/selectionpolicytoolkit/intellectualfreedom.

ALA. 2025. "American Library Association Kicks Off National Library Week with the Top 10 Most Challenged Books of 2024 and the State of America's Libraries Report." News release, April 7. www.ala.org/news/2025/04/american-library-association-kicks-national-library-week-top-10-most-challenged-books.

Berens, Kathi Inman, and Rachel Noorda. 2023. *Gen Z and Millennials: How They Use Public Libraries and Identify through Media Use.* American Library Association. www.ala.org/sites/default/files/advocacy/content/tools/Gen-Z-and-Millennials-Report%20%281%29.pdf.

Blake, Suzanne. 2024. "Florida Under Fire After Kicking 1.8 Million People Off Medicaid." *Newsweek.* https://www.newsweek.com/florida-under-fire-after-kicking-off-1-8-million-medicaid-1923899.

Diamond, Larry, Marc F. Plattner, and Christopher Walker. 2016. *Authoritarianism Goes Global: The Challenge to Democracy.* Johns Hopkins University Press.

Eubanks, Virginia. 2018. *Automating Inequality: How High-Tech Tools Profile, Police, and Punish the Poor.* St. Martin's Press.

Gorman, Michael. 2000. *Our Enduring Values: Librarianship in the 21st Century.* American Library Association.

Hurley, David A., Sarah R. Kostelecky, and Lori Townsend. 2022. *Cultural Humility.* American Library Association.

Khalil, Ashraf. 2022. "Steve Bannon Convicted on Contempt Charges for Defying Jan. 6 Committee Subpoena." *PBS NewsHour.* July 22. www.pbs.org/newshour/politics/steve-bannon-convicted-on-contempt-charges-for-defying-jan-6-committee-subpoena.

Moody, Josh. 2024. "New College of Florida Abruptly Dismisses Librarian." Inside Higher Ed. May 4. www.insidehighered.com/news/quicktakes/2023/05/04/new-college-florida-abruptly-dismisses-librarian.

O'Donnell, Christopher. 2023. "Feds Say Florida Is Failing to Help Many at Risk of Losing Medicaid." *Tampa Bay Times.* August 17. www.tampabay.com/news/health/2023/08/17/medicaid-florida-enrollment-dcf/.

Storytelling Against Library Misinformation

Over twenty years ago, in a small town in the Midwest, there was a library board tasked with approving plans for a long-awaited building expansion. Building renovations should be a routine occurrence for libraries, but in fact, recent data shows that 40 percent of library buildings have not been renovated since 2000 or earlier (Goek 2023). In this case, the building renovation plans looked complete, and the board was almost ready to vote and send the plans up to the city council.

But there was a catch. In a secret meeting, the mayor demanded that the library director change the building plans, and reduce the square footage of the planned expansion by almost 25 percent. The library director was told to tell no one, not even the board who would be voting, or else he would be fired. Large amounts of data, like highly detailed blueprints, can be overwhelming, and the mayor was counting on no one noticing the last-minute changes. Fortunately, the library director spoke with trusted staff members in the administrative office, and word got back to the city council that the plans had been altered without a public process. Then library board members were alerted. City officials demanded to see the original plans, with the original square footage. Stakeholders at all levels are obligated, for the good of public and institutional resources, to ask detailed questions about proposals for major renovations. Thanks to motivated public officials and a budget that could handle the expansion, the originally planned renovations were completed. That building stands today, serving a busy community of library lovers.

While examples like these must remain anonymous, the deliberate presentation of inaccurate information for political reasons is not new, nor is it an isolated incident. Boards of trustees and citizens may have different perspectives on their library, but everyone should be able to tell stories about the library that are grounded in accurate data. Misinformation about libraries, however, is abundant. Libraries must navigate a digital world where large right-wing activist groups misrepresent library data and missions (Magnusson 2024), and bots now comprise almost half of internet traffic, with malicious bots comprising a third of them (Woollacott 2024). Misinformation is a live issue with real cultural, political, and practical implications for library workers around the world today (IFLA 2023; European Commission, n.d.; Universitat Oberta de Catalunya 2022; Vancouver Public Library, n.d.; Yarra Plenty Regional Library 2021).

This chapter defines *library misinformation* in relation to common processes of the evolution of libraries and their communities, from building renovations to book collections. It also defines and explores *misinformation* as a dynamic process of retelling (and often exaggerating) false stories, drawing on lessons learned from resisting historical tyranny. A critical lens focuses on who has power or stands to gain power from certain library misinformation tactics. Currently, library workers committed to measured debate and collaboration are routinely losing power when faced with strategies designed to distract and confuse and, ultimately, to destroy intellectual freedom and defund libraries. Because of the limitations of civil processes in the face of censors exercising raw power to force their specific morals on the public, this chapter concludes with a step-by-step guide to assess a misinformation campaign against a library and how to take action.

Defining Misinformation, Disinformation, and Malinformation

Bad information poses threats to many aspects of daily life, from voting to health care. In her widely referenced work on "information disorder," Claire Wardle (2020) defines misinformation in relation to disinformation and malinformation.

Misinformation is false, misleading, or inaccurate information shared by someone unaware who thinks they are helping (Wardle 2020). For example, a person might spread what is actually a fake news story while believing that they are sharing something that is true or accurate. Misinformation can also be a rumor or gossip generated by the normal human tendency to exaggerate, misremember, or recall only selected details. Taken out of context, the interpretation of a fact can also become misinformation, as when a pay discrepancy is attributed to merit, but the pattern of compensation across the organization reveals systemic lower compensation for women and people of color. *Misinformation* is a useful label when it is unclear whether a person knows that the information they're sharing is false or not.

By contrast, *disinformation* is false information that is deliberately shared with the intent to cause harm (Wardle 2020). It is usually created to make money, influence people's political beliefs, or manipulate the public in some other way. Disinformation happens, for example, when a book-banning group launches a "personal smear campaign" with false allegations about a librarian because they dislike her storytime book choices (Carey 2024). It is frightening but essential for librarians to be aware how much more quickly false stories travel than true ones (Vosoughi et al. 2018). In addition to human-generated disinformation, bots and artificial intelligence systems also generate disinformation and can rapidly spread fake news, and there is currently no clear solution to this (Ruffo et al. 2023). Disinformation created to cause harm becomes misinformation when it is re-shared by someone who does not know that it is false, and this innocent re-sharing amplifies the harm.

Finally, *malinformation* is genuine information that is spread with the intent to cause harm (Wardle 2020). Malinformation occurs, for example, when a person tells a story about a coworker's mistake, revealing that mistake to others and harming the coworker's reputation without giving the coworker a chance to fix the mistake or explain how it happened. Malinformation has also been defined as racism in action, such as when peaceful protests against racism are mischaracterized by white supremacist groups as violent in order to discredit the protestors (Cooke 2021).

Misinformation matters most in a specific context, where inaccurate rumors are amplified by disinformation designed to confuse or mislead people. In the library example discussed at the start of this chapter, the mayor created *disinformation* about the library renovation plans to try to save the city money, and this intentionally false information became *misinformation* when those plans went forward to the board and council, who were unaware of the changes. The mayor planned to spread *malinformation* when he threatened to fire the library director if the director revealed the truth. Fortunately, library staff overheard the conversation and the truth prevailed. The misinformation was corrected, the source of the disinformation was revealed, the malinformation did not spread, and in the end, that mayor was not reelected. But not all situations are so fortunate. Since the COVID-19 pandemic in 2020, the misinformation surrounding the virus has provided a harrowing example of how misinformation can cause harm, with some data storytelling lessons for libraries.

Inside an Infodemic

In spring 2021, I was asked to give a presentation about storytelling to a group of researchers, many of them medical scientists and former doctors, who were working at global policy levels to respond to the COVID-19 pandemic and related misinformation. They were grappling with the problems in COVID-19 communication that became known as the "infodemic." An infodemic occurs when the public's overwhelming concern and interest in a disease outbreak (or some other issue) generates an onslaught of information, some of it accurate and some of it inaccurate. This overabundance proves a fertile ground for both misinformation and deliberately crafted disinformation to thrive (World Health Organization 2021). Disinformation in the COVID-19 era included false stories about vaccine contents and their consequences, government intentions in vaccination programs, how airborne viruses spread, and more.

For my storytelling presentation, the task was to help find ways to detect viral misinformation and develop a rapid way to provide front-line public health workers—whose information roles in an infodemic are remarkably like library workers' information literacy work—with accurate information packaged for easy distribution. Figure 5.1 shows the use of storytelling concepts to help build clear stories that could carry accurate information to public health workers, who could then retell these stories to audiences in their local languages across the Americas (Brooks et al. 2023).

This work led to the analysis of several stories in relation to their narrative strategies, with a focus on what goes wrong with information in a story retelling process. Specifically, the same classic narrative structures that help us to tell stories well, from chapter 3, can be misused to perpetuate misinformation. For example, disinformation about ineffective COVID-19 treatments (light therapy, veterinary de-worming medications, drinking poison, etc.) may be couched as a "secret" shared between teller and audience who are allied against an unnamed "them" and "what they're not telling you." At the same time, public health organizations trying to promote new vaccines may have much to learn about medical racism because many people have family members who have been

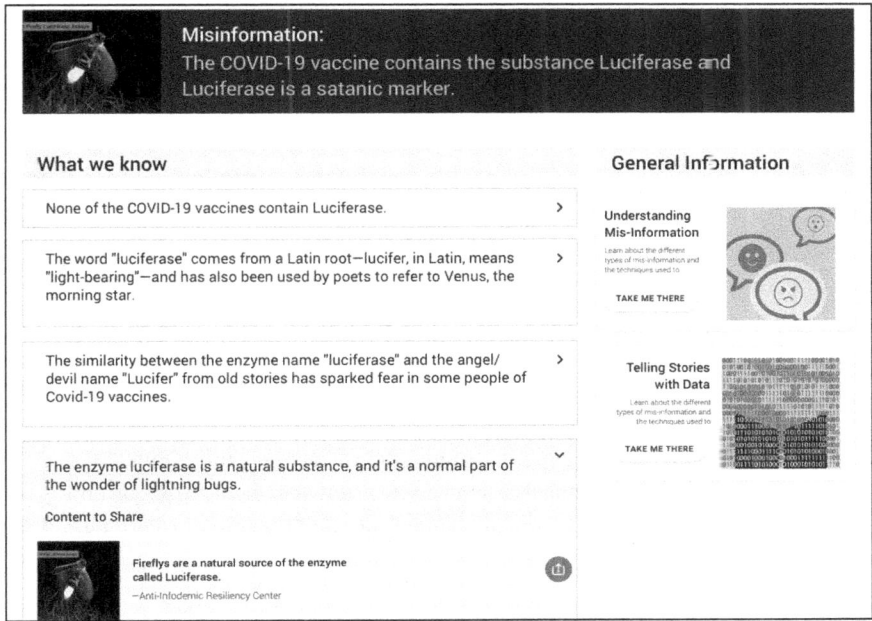

FIGURE 5.1
Debunking misinformation for public health

Source: Brooks et al. 2023

subjected to malicious medical trauma and genocides, such as the Tuskegee syphilis experiments (Howell 2005), and consequently do not trust vaccines or medical science. Navigating the aftermath of historical abuse or exploitation requires thoughtful approaches, not simply the provision of more information (McDowell 2024). The COVID-19 pandemic and its accompanying infodemic have provided an ongoing case for understanding what can go wrong with information, and this infodemic work can point to strategies for overcoming misinformation and related communication breakdowns in libraries.

Lessons for Libraries from an Infodemic

Features of a Library Infodemic

First, the bad news: Libraries are in trouble too. The overwhelming concern and confusion of an infodemic can happen anytime, not just during a pandemic.

Currently, we live in a confused and confusing time regarding what it means to have free access to information. In the United States, we are witnessing the highest levels of organized book-banning activism ever recorded. Unfortunately, censorship is one manifestation of right-wing authoritarianism, which is becoming a global problem. Along with new forms of intellectual restriction, disinformation is rampant online and threatens "freedom of thought, the right to privacy and the right to democratic participation, as well as endangering a range of economic, social and cultural rights" (Colomina et al. 2021). A recent European Union report described the increase in polarization and disinformation since 2020 this way:

> [The COVID-19 pandemic] has unleashed new, more intense and increasingly varied disinformation campaigns around the world. Many non-democratic regimes have made use of the pandemic to crack down on political opposition by restricting freedom of expression and freedom of the media. COVID-19 compounds both disinformation's threat to international human rights, on the one hand, and the dangers of counter-disinformation serving anti-democratic agendas, on the other. (Colomina et al. 2021)

The World Health Organization also touched on misinformation from the COVID-inspired infodemic, stating that "the technology we rely on to keep connected and informed is enabling and amplifying an infodemic that continues to undermine the global response and jeopardizes measures to control the pandemic" (World Health Organization 2020).

We routinely read news about attacks on the mission and funding of public libraries, the blaming and dehumanizing of librarians, and related messaging about other public institutions, such as questioning the need for public broadcasting media. We daily encounter wild rumors about information institutions that, just a few years ago, seemed cherished and valued as civic spaces in a democratic society. Disinformation has taken hold of people's imaginations in deeply troubling ways, and libraries and their commitment to principles of intellectual freedom are under active attack by authoritarian leaders and groups.

Some of the main features of the infodemic about libraries are the following:

- "Parents' rights" groups are spreading homophobic and racist viewpoints and are generalizing their goals for their own children to all of us, regardless of the diverse identities and viewpoints that exist outside their echo chamber.

- Library workers are being criminalized for not censoring people's access to information, thereby promoting discriminatory views of right-wing activists.
- Conservative activist groups and legislators are targeting school and public libraries with calls for book banning, and in some states, they are tying libraries' funding to "book restrictions" (Chapoco 2024; Harris and Alter 2023).

Book Banning and Challenges in the United States

According to the ALA's Office for Intellectual Freedom (OIF), which has tracked and reported book challenges and bans in the United States since 1990, most challenged books are by or about people of color or LGBTQ.A+ people. Data collected in recent years indicates that the infodemic is connected to a surge in censorship.

- In 2024, there were 821 attempts to censor library materials and services and documented challenges to 2,452 unique titles.
- In 2023, there were 1,247 attempts to censor library materials and services and documented challenges to 4,240 unique titles.
- In 2022, there were 681 attempts to ban or restrict library resources, challenging 1,651 unique titles.
- In 2021, there were 729 attempts to censor library resources, challenging 1,597 unique titles.

Since 2021, most years have seen the highest numbers of attempted book bans since the OIF began collecting data thirty-five years ago. Challenges to unique titles increased significantly from 2022 to 2023, and the numbers for 2024 are lower only due to whole states supporting censorship, which has decreased local censorship attempts there (ALA 2023; ALA 2025). According to ALA, "pressure groups and government entities that included elected officials, board members, and administrators initiated 72% of demands to censor books in school and public libraries" (ALA 2025).

While the information overload on the internet has amplified the library infodemic, it is made even more serious by the activities of pro-censorship groups with authoritarian tendencies, which are not unique to the United States (Silver and Fetterolf 2024). From book banning to impacts on library workers, this infodemic affects the work we do, and thus requires ever clearer explanations of intellectual freedom and professional ethics to library workers, patrons, boards, and community partners alike.

Effects of Right-Wing Activism on Intellectual Freedom

Because of its impact, it is worth exploring some of the features of pro-censorship right-wing activism. What motivates people to ban books, especially in an era of nearly ubiquitous access to information via the internet? Emily Knox, the foremost expert on contemporary US book censorship, has been studying this topic for over a decade. Writing in *Book Banning in 21st-Century America*, Knox defined the core issues:

> The discourse of censorship can be understood as a discourse of both anxiety and action. It focuses on the reasons why certain types of knowledge should not be made available to a particular population and is rooted in many different spheres. Challengers employ arguments from religious and scientific domains as well as a foundation regarding the power of books and reading. (Knox 2015, 137)

Historically speaking, it is not surprising that book banning would arise in these times, as a "lagging indicator" of the growing cultural anxiety aroused by rapidly changing technologies and more. It is also important to understand that book challenges are symbolic. "Book challengers are attempting to both make a statement and effect change within their communities' institutions through their actions; namely, they are trying to ensure that these institutions reflect their own values," especially as they relate to children (Knox 2015, 121).

Many local news stories bear out these dynamics of anxiety and action. For instance, Angie Hayden, the founder of Read Freely Alabama, describes the pro-censorship rhetoric of an activist group in Alabama:

> Their entire tactic is to get people so afraid that these books are coming for their children, that there's some sort of agenda coming for their children when really the library is just a place for all sorts of viewpoints that represent all sorts of people. (Morris 2024)

Although this may not be surprising from a historical perspective, it is still deeply affecting for those who understand the value of libraries to experience this wave of challenges. Book challenges are also followed by censorship of research databases, as in Mississippi where databases have been scrubbed of the now illegal terms "race relations" and "gender studies" (Goldberg and Wilder 2025).

To stand up for intellectual freedom, it is necessary to have a clear definition of what censorship is:

> Censorship is an act of control, driven by a combustible mix of power, privilege, and fear. Large pro-censorship movements historically occur in response to social changes that alarm a privileged population, with the goal of dictating access to information for the entire community that is in accord with the personal beliefs of the privileged group. The urge to censor is rooted in the use of raw power to preserve the currently privileged, and censorship will be a threat to libraries as long as privilege seeks to perpetuate itself. (Jaeger et al. 2023, 1)

This is a critical approach to understanding censorship because it considers the alignment of privilege with power. It fits the current situation well, given that a select group of entitled white activists seeks to impose their morality, and to erase the representations of groups—BIPOC and LGBTQIA+ people—that they dehumanize in their rhetoric. The specific ways of dehumanizing groups can vary, and yet it remains important to name the power, misplaced morality, and dehumanization for what it is. Inequities accumulate for those who hold multiple identities that are under attack. This has a direct impact on library workers, particularly those who hold marginalized identities.

The exercise of raw power now operates to criminalize librarians for doing their jobs (Williamson 2024). Consider the disproportionate impacts on library workers who already face disproportionate odds of incarceration, for themselves and their families (Alexander 2010). If these attacks and new laws persist, will people at disproportionate risk be willing to work in libraries, where professional ethics clash with the personal beliefs of the privileged codified as law? The consequence for the public is the erasure of the representation of whole segments of society. This happens when book banning is successful, but it also happens when materials become less accessible as school libraries attempt to avoid conflict and voluntarily move "certain titles to higher age groups or require parental approval" to borrow them (Italie and Kruesi 2024).

Reframing the Library Infodemic through the Lens of Misinformation

The only way to begin to address all this bad news is to establish a way to think systematically about what is going wrong. When we gain clarity on the problems, we can begin to consider what libraries can do to contribute to solutions. Gaining clarity requires reframing pro-censorship activism in infodemic terms. The elements of book banning and censorship can be reframed as a library-focused infodemic with components of misinformation, disinformation, and malinformation:

- Misinformation includes the idea that children's reading choices are up to librarians rather than parents and the children themselves. Misinformation also includes the idea that libraries should cater to one group rather than to all community members and should offer preconceived ideas about the people that children will grow up to be, possibly different from their parents.
- Disinformation includes accusations that librarians intend to harm children by providing books and other resources that represent a broad range of diverse perspectives. Disinformation includes arguments that books about and written from diverse viewpoints cause harm to children. For example, despite longstanding research showing that very young children already understand racial biases (Cristol and Gimbert 2008), this disinformation argues that white children will be "harmed" by learning about racial injustice because it will disrupt their "innocence" of such inequities.
- Malinformation includes personal attacks against library professionals, such as claims that librarians are part of an evil profession because they seek to corrupt children by, among other things, exposing them to various gender expressions and sexual orientations. Malinformation recasts diversity and intellectual freedom for all as "corruption of the innocent" rather than as opportunities for lifelong learning. Malinformation has sparked some libraries, systems, some state-level library professional organizations to disaffiliate from the American Library Association (Holmes 2023), with other proposals under consideration (Suppe 2023). Some state legislatures have passed laws outlawing affiliation with the ALA in the state (Jensen 2024).

In these difficult times, it becomes increasingly important to tell clear and well-evidenced data stories about the positive impact of libraries. This storytelling can contribute to reversing the current infodemic crisis affecting libraries, especially when stories are focused on serving and motivating local communities. And yet stories alone, however true and well-crafted, cannot solve the global issue of misinformation and its local impacts. The global reach of online disinformation is *designed* to create outrage and distraction. Engaging in point-by-point responses to "tell the story" is readily outscaled by bots, and their social media illusion of meaningful participation that robs people of the clarity and focus needed to defend democracy (and libraries). We should recall the local library director whom the mayor threatened; just "telling the story" would have resulted in the director's termination, and the mayor probably would have forced the next director to carry out the deception. For library advocates to stay motivated to act, it is important to find strategic and practical grounds on which to base a stance against censorship.

Lessons on Tyranny for Libraries: Toward a Practical Stance against Censorship

Standing up to censorship requires intellectual and emotional strength. Gaining perspective on these disturbing times is possible if we step back and consider other times and places where raw power was exercised. Chapter 4 mentions the renewed interest in twentieth-century totalitarian movements. In his book *On Tyranny: Twenty Lessons from the 20th Century*, Timothy Snyder (2017) outlines takeaways from the systematic genocides conducted during World War II. Snyder's twenty lessons cover many of the cultural and social nuances of resistance and survival during such times of tyranny, including the historical lead-up to authoritarian, totalitarian, and fascist regimes. With regard to contemporary book banning in the United States, the following list adapts five selected lessons from Snyder's work to address libraries.

1. Do not obey in advance.
2. Defend institutions.
3. Remember professional ethics.
4. Notice shifting language.
5. Make eye contact and small talk.

These five lessons, explored in detail in the following sections, highlight the importance of library work and how it can be most effective in protecting people and the political freedoms of democracy.

Do Not Obey in Advance

If a library's collection policies continue to state that all viewpoints will be represented in its materials, but the chilling effect of censorship efforts means that librarians purchase less of what they predict might be controversial, then the collections will suffer. If programs are canceled to avoid protests, communities lose the opportunity to hear diverse points of view. If libraries try to placate a small number of angry citizens by removing representations of minority or other marginalized community members from collections or programs, then children cannot see themselves and their families represented in the library. Many librarians will obey in advance when facing the highest level of censorship ever recorded in US library history, and we should strive to forgive each other while remembering that it is worth resisting. Obeying in advance of future threats simply gives those making the threats more power. Attempting to placate will not prevent the raw exercise of power and the discrimination of the powerful. Carry on as usual, get through conflicts as they arise, and do not obey in advance.

Defend Institutions

Telling library data stories is not just for annual budgets or reports. The more informed people are, from elected representatives to the general public, the easier it will be to defend libraries as institutions. Defending institutions requires a commitment to learn and to act. Effective data storytelling allows people to learn what the library accomplishes, both daily and over time. For example, while histories of libraries are important stories about how those institutions have navigated change in the past, they are also rich sources of data about the libraries' impact over time. Library impact is measured in many ways, through both formal data collection and anecdotal experiences.

When it comes to defending institutions, all forms of data are worth collecting. When people have learned what the library is, does, and has done, then they are positioned to act by speaking up about its value and voting to support it. In difficult times, the most fraught decisions are those that involve how to defend libraries as institutions without inflaming the opposition calling for their destruction, through politics or violence (Cloonan 2018). Such complex judgment calls are local but have a global impact because the defense of institutions is the only way that future generations will have libraries.

Remember Professional Ethics

Librarians have produced some of the most important professional ethics statements about intellectual freedom. For example, the ALA Code of Ethics, which dates to 1939, lists principles related to the ethical provision of library services. The second statement in the code reads: "We uphold the principles of intellectual freedom and resist all effort to censor library resources" (ALA 2021).

A longstanding commitment to intellectual freedom and professional ethics has sustained LIS professionals through every kind of political context thanks to the diligent efforts of library workers. As a professional organization, the ALA has survived both recent and historical disaffiliations. Conflicts about the meaning of true equity and inclusion have resurged in recent years, just as they did in the Jim Crow and the Civil Rights eras in the early to mid-twentieth century (Nappo 2024). Whether a particular library or region is affiliated with the ALA or not, generations of library professionals have adhered to the ALA Code of Ethics, the Core Values of Librarianship (ALA 2024a), and more specialized statements of professional ethics, such as values for teen services (YALSA 2015), rare book and manuscript collections (ACRL Rare Books and Manuscripts Section 2020), and many others. These statements can inform library work at every level and in every library staff position. Know those statements, read them, discuss them, and let them be a set of ideals that inform the real practices of everyday library work.

Notice Shifting Language

Staying informed is important, and in times of upheaval, it is easy to get lost in the noise of the news. Snyder recommends reading anything that provokes us to think, and remaining attentive to the shifting language that is used around us. Otherwise, each story is "breaking" news, only to be displaced by the next one: "So we are hit by wave upon wave but never see the ocean" (Snyder 2017, 52). Noticing shifts in language means noticing the nuances, including how certain phrases like "protect our children" reject any legitimate opposition. Book-banning groups use words like *freedom* and *safety* without saying what these words do, which is to block the freedom to read through censorship.

We must identify what is happening and seek a larger framework for understanding the events around us, one in which changing language does not strip us of the power to think systematically about the reality of what is being done. Recall that, in one poll, about a third of Americans were unaware that the Affordable Care Act was the same thing as Obamacare, the name used by Republicans to delegitimize this historic health care legislation by activating hatred of President Obama (Dropp and Nyhan 2017). Surviving tyranny requires clear thinking, which is supported by noticing shifting language.

Make Eye Contact and Small Talk

As discussed in chapter 4, polarized audiences have no common ground from which to build a consensus. Cultivating common ground means preserving the possibility of connection. Politeness, in these contexts, is not simple or banal but instead is a strategic way of continuing to signal our shared humanity—as distinct from totalitarian dehumanization. It is expressed by small gestures that vary from culture to culture, but in the US library context, those gestures include a nod, wave, smile, saying hello, commenting about the weather, and more. These may be intended as small kindnesses, but they are also a strategic way to represent the library as an institution worth defending for its equitable inclusion of all. While it may be tempting to disengage during times of stress, making eye contact, small talk, and any other gesture acknowledging our shared humanity is important because these build the possibility of common ground.

Addressing Polarized Audiences in Infodemic Times

One of the most difficult aspects of data storytelling arises in times when polarized audiences are both incorrect and behaving in uncivil ways. Audiences who have been primed with fake data or false interpretations of that data are wrong or misinformed. Audiences who combine wrong information with shaming, blaming, and inflammatory attacks in attempts to impose their morality on everyone are behaving in uncivil ways. By developing our own internal landscape of logical resilience in the face of manipulative messaging, library advocates can conserve energy to connect with and persuade wrong and mean audiences (see box 5.1).

BOX 5.1

Naming the Issues, Instead of Using "Fighting Words"

The internal conversations among library staff are often very different from those staffers' external messaging. Consider a situation where a library patron requires or requests more time than the reference staff can give. A patron who needs more individual attention than staff have time to offer will need clear messaging and redirection to more independent ways to meet their needs.

Staff will talk among themselves, and they may use words to name the issues—the patron behaves in self-absorbed ways, interrupts when being offered resources, or changes the subject to keep the conversation going—that are never intended for the patron to hear. Naming the issues at play, such as when a group is behaving badly or improperly, is a necessary part of the strategizing process. These are not *fighting words;* rather, they are words used in the privacy of staff deliberations to respectfully understand the issues at play. When it comes to people, the focus should always remain on their *behavior,* not on their personal attributes. Who they are is unknown to us; we are only able to judge them by their behavior. When it is necessary to judge behavior, staff should consult among themselves and then communicate in the most peaceful and de-escalating way possible.

Developing a clear logical stance in relation to defending intellectual freedom is a skill. A logical stance must draw from values statements, principles, professional ethics, and practices based in librarianship. It must be anchored in the larger understanding that libraries support democracy by protecting people's freedom to explore ideas, access information, and build knowledge. Cultivating an understanding of the logic of intellectual freedom provides a kind of armor when a library is under attack from pro-censorship groups. Logic prepares us to think clearly about what we are doing and why we are doing it. This is especially important when a local community is flooded with misinformation, impacting meetings and conversations. Awareness can help slow down an escalating conflict by providing strategic ways to respond.

In the face of polarized audiences and divergent cultural perspectives, aiming to win an argument—by proving your view is right—is unlikely to be an effective way forward. In such situations, it becomes important to recognize the limits of argumentation, while at the same time developing a practical strategy to sustain the library's mission as much as possible. Recall the steps to address *polarized audiences* from the previous chapter:

- Identify the problem.
- Determine what to do about the problem.
- Determine when to persuade and when to avoid debate.
- Stay on message.

Let's take each of these steps in turn.

Identifying the Problem

Identifying a library infodemic problem means thinking carefully about the issues, people, and rhetoric being used. We must seek to understand as much about the problem as possible, both the literal complaints or proposals raised against the library and what these symbolize. It also means understanding what is at stake related to the library's purpose. If proposals to limit access, strip collections, or otherwise diminish the library are successful, then who stands to lose? And what will they lose? How would such proposals impact the future of the community? How does the problem relate to people's opinions and cultural identities? What anxieties are at play? Identifying the problem takes time outside of confrontational spaces. Avoid "both sides" rhetorical traps, in which there can seem to be only two opposing sides to many issues, rather than many varied constituents whom the library serves.

Identifying the problem is usually difficult, as anxiety-based rhetoric often interweaves proposals with outrage and evidence designed to shock audiences. Leaders will be faced with the anxieties of library staff and the need to ensure that their rights are protected. It is vital, however, to identify allies who can engage in analysis of the problem even while under attack. Allies can help us find the right words and phrases to identify the problem, such as censorship, scapegoating, or misinformation, and name what is wrong without blaming the audience. There is good reason for this strategy, as many of those who perpetuate misinformation do so unwittingly (Starbird et al. 2023). This nonviolent rhetoric is more than symbolic because it is also a path to calling on audiences to act (McDowell and Cooke 2022).

Two examples of problems will illustrate some strategies for identifying them: *disinformation blueprints* and *book banning*.

Disinformation blueprints. In the story that opened this chapter, the library board discovered that alterations to blueprints had been made without their approval. Identifying the problem was a process of comparing the previously approved specifications with the current blueprints. At stake was the expense of the renovation, which left the board with only a few people at the city administrative level who had the ability and motivation to secretly alter the blueprints.

Book banning. In a typical case of contemporary book banning, the problem will begin with a challenge to books in a library, often a list of a hundred or so books at a time. In some cases, libraries do not have these books in their collection to begin with, so identifying the problem includes understanding where the list came from, which is often from a national book-banning organization, such as Moms for Liberty. Identifying the problem includes understanding which books the library owns specifically and researching the rhetoric of book banning generally, as well as the affiliations of any local actors with national groups.

Determining What to Do About the Problem

When opposing value systems amplified by the strategies of right-wing disinformation activism collide, tensions will be high. Determining what to do about infodemic problems requires many considerations. Is there common ground? If so, we must find it. If the goal is the expression of values, are there ways that the library can demonstrate that it already reflects those values in many areas of the collection? At a local level, established relationships might present a way forward.

The context of book banning as an organized group activity, however, may preclude local solutions. Remember that the ultimate purpose of the library is to open doors to freedom. Read Freely Alabama, a citizens group formed to counter pro-censorship activities, released a statement that personalized the impacts of censorship and the freedom found at the library: "Many of us grew up poor, in marginalized communities and secretly closeted in these very towns, with the public library as the only way we could access books for free" (Albanese 2024). While this statement provides one example of clarity about why libraries must take action in infodemic times, remember that determining what specific action to take is always deeply contextual. Revisiting the two examples introduced above (disinformation blueprints and book banning) will provide a sense of different ways to address a local infodemic problem.

Disinformation Blueprints

Determining what to do about a dishonest mayor who is misrepresenting library expansion plans and threatening a library director involves the consideration of multiple factors. The library director may choose to activate a network of trusted colleagues for strategic consultation. In a case where the library director has been instructed not to communicate the blueprint modifications to the library board, speaking out publicly against the mayor would lead to retaliation. It becomes important to find other ways to spread the word that something is wrong, including considering who among the staff might have trusted relationships through which they could spread the word to city officials.

The goal is to communicate the reality of the situation, but the strategy must include understanding more about why this is happening and who supports a smaller library footprint, which is most likely based on a disagreement about how public money should be spent. Options for what to do include researching similar expansion footprints and investments, asking for help to understand whose interests are at play, and making some strategic communication decisions to find out more about what is happening and why.

If the library director is not free to speak publicly, then it may be important to determine who else would be free to speak with city representatives, which might include library staff, board members, or elected representatives who determine library funding. If city officials are unaware of the changes, they may spark further investigation without any involvement from the library director. Once efforts are underway to correct the misinformation, the director can support these efforts at the next library board meeting, inviting any questions about the process of planning for expansion. In any case in which elected officials are misrepresenting or selectively representing facts to the public, such as the planned footprint of a new building, this kind of complex process of activating networks of allies is likely to be required.

Book Banning

Determining what to do about a book-banning threat depends on the community. The goal is to ensure that libraries reflect broadly inclusive community values through their books and other resources. The challenge is to predict what the community will work to defend, sometimes by counting the likely votes on a board or the likely voters in an election. Every element of knowing the audience—demographics, their knowledge of libraries, their attitudes, and any other available data—will be important to collect and analyze to predict whether a community will defend the inclusive mission of the library, support book banning, or be indifferent.

Crafting a message of respect and inclusion will be necessary and may even be effective because libraries are often highly trusted institutions (EveryLibrary Institute 2023). Some options for messaging in infodemic times include:

- Naming the positive values that libraries bring to all members of the community
- Demonstrating how the library's collections reflect the values of all community members, including those who challenge books
- Stating the negative impacts of censorship on a community
- Establishing or following the library's formal selection and reconsideration policies

When hundreds of books are challenged at once, the library can follow its reconsideration policy; this will take time, and it could potentially limit or slow down the local conflict. For example, the library's reconsideration policy can limit who may challenge a book to only local community members. The policy can also require a separate form for each book being challenged. It can establish that reconsideration committee decisions are binding for a period of time. For example, "your policy could say that the decision of a reconsideration committee is binding for three years, after which it may be considered again" (Calzada et al. 2024). For many book challenge situations, the ALA's "Selection & Reconsideration Policy Toolkit for Public, School, & Academic Libraries" (ALA 2018) will be invaluable, along with supporting resources like the Unite Against Book Bans website (ALA 2024b) and the Get Ready, Stay Ready Toolkit (Byrd Fort et al. 2022). (More on these resources appears in the "Staying on Message" section later in this chapter.)

Unfortunately, if misinformation has already inflamed the community, then any of these messages could further polarize the audience. Libraries must strive to understand how their communities depend on them and predict whether they will defend the inclusive mission of the library, even when librarians themselves are under attack (see box 5.2).

BOX 5.2
What about Personal Attacks?

The reality is that, nationally and locally, personal attacks against individuals or groups have increased. This includes scapegoating attacks, such as when LGBTQIA+ people are lumped into one group and treated as the enemies of children, when in fact people in the LGBTQIA+ community have families and children themselves. Recently, children's librarians have been personally and professionally attacked with absurd claims meant to demonize them through accusations of causing mental and sexual harm and trauma to children. Library leaders are also attacked routinely now, in the press and social media.

Library advocates must prepare strategies for personal attacks. A few key steps to address personal attacks made on social media, in the press, or in a meeting include:

- Point out what is happening, clearly and with minimal expressiveness. Use phrases like, "That's a personal attack, that's not what we're here to discuss," or "We are here to talk about the library, we need to focus on the issues at hand, so please stop these personal attacks." Stay calm, slow down, and say clearly what has just transpired.
- Don't take the bait. Never repeat an absurd negative claim meant to scapegoat an individual or group. This includes refutation, as in "That's not true, we are not all _ _ _ _ _." The problem with any response that repeats the accusation is that the audience hears you repeat the very same claim that the attackers made. Do not amplify their message by repeating it, and avoid sounding or looking defensive.
- Prepare and practice. Be creative and ready with words and phrases that can deflect, lightly if possible. Consider acknowledging the underlying anxiety without engaging the specific accusations. Here's an example: "I hear that you are deeply concerned, but we will not entertain personal

attacks." (More on de-escalation is discussed in the "Staying on Message" section later in this chapter.)

- Redirect the discussion to the topic at hand with phrases like, "We were discussing this proposal, and we need to put aside personal attacks and get back to the substance of the proposal."

Finally, be aware that personal attacks are meant to exploit vulnerabilities. People with multiple marginalized identities are routinely attacked first, the loudest, and the longest. Stand together. Stand up for the right of all participants to engage in civil governance processes. The library belongs to the whole community, and standing up against personal attacks, which are a form of bullying, will make the whole community safer in the long run. Let the story of the conflict be a resounding sense that, at least at the library, we will treat one another with dignity.

Determining When to Persuade and When to Avoid Debate

Determining when to persuade and when to avoid debate comes down to an understanding of intention. Looking back at the categorization of audience attitudes in chapter 4, any time an audience has negative, mixed, or indifferent attitudes, persuasion is reasonable to try. In these situations, the audience is willing to work together, even if they disagree. Data storytelling is a way of communicating an insight based on data analysis to an audience to persuade them to see the same interpretation as the storyteller. Story is important because it not only makes the insight memorable but also makes it possible for an audience to explain to other audiences—whether the constituents of an elected representative or other community members—why they have been persuaded to agree with that interpretation. If a voting majority of a board holds attitudes based on a shared reality, then persuasion has potential.

If a significant subset of a board holds polarized attitudes and does not share the same reality, however, avoiding attempts to persuade them is often the wiser course. For example, people may seek election to a board to defund the library because they believe that it is harming children. Years' worth of credible research indicates that libraries are actually a key factor in educational success, from the earliest school libraries all the way through college (SLIDE 2024; Brown and Malenfant 2017; Lance 1994). The idea that loaning books that represent diverse perspectives causes harm to children stands in opposition to clear findings that libraries support learning. A polarized audience, however, is more likely to be inflamed by disagreement, deflecting and distracting from the issue at hand with ever more shocking claims.

Polarized audiences adhere to a different reality, one in which their morality alone is viable, and all others should adhere to their values. Engaging in direct debate, and especially attempting to refute points, is not effective in these situations. Like persuasion, debate will either enrage such an audience or offer them an opportunity to undermine opposing viewpoints. As the Moms for Liberty website states, if they can't "hold accountable" leaders who disagree with them, then "we work to replace them with liberty-minded individuals" (Moms for Liberty 2024). Notice the shifting language here: The use of the word "liberty" in this context has little to do with its dictionary definition.

Persuasion, debate, or appeal to common goals and values will fail in the face of organized groups who are trained to use such rhetoric to shame, blame, and inflame. The only reasonable approach is to avoid debate and stay on message, as discussed later in this chapter in the "Stay on Message" section.

Disinformation Blueprints

As stated previously, a direct debate between the library director and the mayor would have resulted not only in heightened community conflict, but probably in the termination of the library director as well. Instead, a trusted library staff member from the administrative offices was able to reach out to a trusted member of the city council. Providing this alert enabled city council members to raise questions about the original version of the library expansion plans and why these had been cut without board approval in later versions. This in turn alerted library board members, who requested an additional opportunity to review the blueprints going up to the city council. The library director followed the mayor's directive to not alert the board (under threat of termination), but the director did not "obey in advance" by remaining silent. By speaking openly with staff in the administrative offices, the library director followed orders, alerted stakeholders, and avoided debating or confronting the mayor.

Book Banning

Current book-banning movements seeks to discredit library staff and libraries as institutions by sowing suspicion, distrust, and blame. Persuasion is unlikely to be successful with such audiences because, as organized groups state, they will attempt to "replace" any library leaders who do not agree with their point of view—library board members included. Since the central claim of most pro-censorship groups rests on parental rights rhetoric, ways for library leaders to avoid debate in these situations include affirming their support of parents reading with their children, guiding their book selection, and encouraging them to read. While one side spouts vitriol, it is possible for library leaders to provide a detailed data story about the perennial success of summer reading programs in preventing learning loss when school is not in session (ALA 2024c). But doing this effectively in the face of strategies designed to create confusion requires a fierce determination to stay on message.

Staying on Message

Staying on message requires having a message, presenting it coherently and consistently, and steadfastly ignoring all attempts to derail it. The exercise of raw power is done by the deliberate creation of confusion through emotional manipulation, hostile attacks, and a variety of intimidation tactics. As mentioned in chapter 4, a well-known disinformation tactic is to "flood the zone" with disinformation and misinformation. Although we aspire to civic well-being in a democracy, we must not allow the exercise of raw power to overwhelm the message of what libraries give to their communities.

When asserting power is the only agenda of a group seeking to impose its personal views and undermine the democratic process, there is little common ground to find. Instead, craft a message and stay on it, no matter what the tone—blaming, shaming, inflaming—and level of the personal attacks, whether in meetings or on social media. It is not impolite to ignore people who are using blaming, shaming, and inflammatory rhetoric to force their beliefs on everyone in a community. And yet it takes practice to stay on message when someone is trying to disrupt the ability of library staff to deliver any message at all. Do not repeat the phrases and catchwords that are used by the groups seeking to defund libraries. And never repeat any insulting words they use about library staff, library values, or about the public.

This approach to staying on message can create feelings of cognitive dissonance, which is one goal of disinformation. Holding to the principles of a reasoned democratic stance is difficult and may require acquiring new de-escalation skills. George Thompson (n.d.), an English professor-turned-police officer, founded Verbal Judo to teach de-escalation techniques. In very heated or violent situations, he advocates taking five steps, adapted here for libraries:

1. *Ask:* Request to connect, respectfully, and try to discern what is really happening.
2. *Set the context:* Explain why it is important to find a way forward and how the democratic process works.
3. *Present options:* Tell people about the democratic process governing the library and how it benefits them to participate.
4. *Confirm:* Use words to create a bridge, for example, by asking: "Is there anything I can say to . . . ," or "I'd like to be able to help you . . ."
5. *Act:* If the conflict continues to escalate, then get assistance from a coworker, disengage, protect yourself, call for help, and so on.

Avoid using language that expresses your personal feelings during conflicts. Do not take it personally; their anger is with the situation, not with you. No matter how intense a confrontation becomes, a librarian stays professional and represents their institution. Strategies for finding a resolution may involve tactical peace phrases, such as:

- May I talk to you?
- What can I do to help?
- Could I ask you . . . ?
- Would you assist me . . . ?
- Can you work with me?

It can be challenging to look at conflict creatively, but expressions of anger—at meetings or in unexpected moments of confrontation—can provide a chance to practice de-escalation. Remaining under emotional control, speaking slowly, speaking peacefully, and other non-threatening gestures will allow us to remain professional, detached, and ready to create peace while staying on message and defending libraries. Let's look at our two examples one final time.

Disinformation Blueprints

Of course, when the mayor learned that his secret changes to the blueprints were being questioned, he was furious. In one meeting, he even threw a chair at a person who was challenging his viewpoint. Luckily, no one was hurt, but word about his uncivil expression of rage traveled around the city. The library board stayed on message, repeating the goal to stick with the originally approved expansion plan. At the next city council meeting, the original version of the library expansion blueprints was approved. And at the next election, that mayor was not reelected.

Book Banning

Name the issue, be clear about what is at stake, and defend the breadth of the library as a place for all community members. Craft a clear message that libraries oppose censorship and support the freedom to read. Reclaim words like *liberty* and *freedom* for their traditional uses in supporting democratic values, such as the right to read freely. Unite with others to stand against book bans (Unite Against Book Bans, n.d.). Use resources like the Get Ready, Stay Ready Toolkit to craft clear messages, and learn from others' experiences while defending libraries (Byrd Fort et al. 2022). The authors of this toolkit presented a panel at the ALA annual conference in 2023. One of the panelists, a lawyer for the ALA, suggested naming the issue this way: "Your group supports book banning, and that's censorship. We don't support censorship; we support the freedom to read." Most importantly, to stay on message, practice de-escalation. Role-play these scenarios ahead of a major public confrontation between censorship groups and library supporters. Be ready to withstand shaming, blaming, and inflammatory rhetoric while staying on message.

Conclusion: Libraries in Infodemic Times

There is no greater indication that libraries have a role to play in a free society than the degree to which they are attacked by authoritarian leaders and pro-censorship groups. Those attacks have immediate, medium-term, and long-term consequences, some of which can be prevented, mitigated, or at least moderated if we learn to define and speak up for the roles that libraries play in society.

The immediate consequences of authoritarianism are deeply felt in communities where the mission of the library and library workers are attacked. Staff and leaders must grapple with the mindset shifts needed to move immediately from an open and welcoming attitude toward the public to defending their professionalism and profession. The medium-term consequences may be harder to quantify and counteract. Some libraries may try to protect their workers by cutting back on programs that now require multiple staff to ensure workplace safety; or they may limit the diversity of their collections by proactively not buying books that could potentially be controversial. The long-term consequences of censorship and anti-library activism include losing government support for libraries. These losses will disproportionately impact communities in areas where children are not able to access diverse viewpoints from other sources.

Storytelling offers some hope, if we can create the most compelling and best-evidenced data stories of library impact. Libraries need data stories that demonstrate their systematic role in supporting communities, strengthening democracy, and protecting intellectual freedom. It falls to us to amplify arguments about the ways that libraries benefit society. For example, from chapter 3, recall that libraries have a powerful story to tell about supporting not only lifelong *learning* but also lifelong *earning* and the average $381,000 more in taxes college graduates pay over their lifetime, which is much higher than those without advanced degrees (APLU, n.d.). Although a specific library's contributions to lifelong earning might be impossible to fully quantify, it is still worth sharing its value in these terms.

Even more in times of crisis, libraries need to stand up. They provide refuge for communities experiencing traumatic losses. Librarians like Scott Bonner in Ferguson, Missouri, Melanie Townsend-Diggs in Baltimore, and Chera Kowalski in Philadelphia have demonstrated the power of "leading with love and hospitality" by keeping library doors open during the aftermath of police brutality against Black men (Cooke 2019). In the United States today, libraries may be the only places left into which a person can walk freely without having to buy or believe something. When applied with a strategic understanding of countering misinformation, data storytelling can help to sustain libraries as institutions in troubled times. A free and democratic future needs libraries to be part of freedom of thought and freedom of assembly for generations to come.

REFERENCES

ACRL Association of College and Research Libraries, Rare Books and Manuscripts Section. 2020. "Code of Ethics for Special Collections Librarians." https://rbms.info/standards/code_of_ethics/.

Albanese, Andrew. 2024. "Freedom to Read Advocates Blast Alabama Library's Ban on LGBTQ Book Purchases. *Publisher's Weekly*. February 23. www.publishersweekly.com/pw/by-topic/industry-news/libraries/article/94431-freedom-to-read-advocates-blast-alabama-library-s-ban-on-lgbtq-book-purchases.html.

Alexander, Michelle. 2010. *The New Jim Crow: Mass Incarceration in the Age of Colorblindness*. New Press.

ALA American Library Association. 2018. "Selection & Reconsideration Policy Toolkit for Public, School, & Academic Libraries." www.ala.org/tools/challengesupport/selectionpolicytoolkit.

ALA. 2021. "ALA Code of Ethics: A Framework of Values and Ethical Responsibilities for the Profession of Librarianship." www.ala.org/tools/ethics.

ALA. 2023. "American Library Association Releases Preliminary Data on 2023 Book Challenges" [Press release]. September 19. www.ala.org/news/press-releases/2023/09/american-library-association-releases-preliminary-data-2023-book-challenges.

ALA. 2024a. "Core Values of Librarianship." www.ala.org/advocacy/advocacy/intfreedom/corevalues.

ALA. 2024b. "Unite Against Book Bans." https://uniteagainstbookbans.org.

ALA. 2024c. "Summer Reading Programs: Research." https://libguides.ala.org/summer-reading/research.

ALA. 2025. "American Library Association Kicks Off National Library Week with the Top 10 Most Challenged Books of 2024 and the State of America's Libraries Report." News release, April 7. www.ala.org/news/2025/04/american-library-association-kicks-national-library-week-top-10-most-challenged-books.

APLU Association of Public & Land-Grant Universities. n.d. "The Value and Benefit of Public Universities." www.aplu.org/our-work/4-policy-and-advocacy/publicuvalues/.

Brooks, Ian, Marcelo D'Agostino, Myrna Marti, Kate McDowell, Felipe Mejia, Miguel Betancourt-Cravioto, et al. 2023. "An Anti-Infodemic Virtual Center for the Americas." *Pan American Journal of Public Health* 47, no. 5. 10.26633/RPSP.2023.5.

Brown, Karen, and Kara J. Malenfant. 2017. "Academic Library Impact on Student Learning and Success: Findings from Assessment in Action Team Projects." Association of College and Research Libraries. https://alair.ala.org/items/94f5534e-a7e9-4aca-aa54-ce5b4a2d8368.

Byrd Fort, Valerie, Stacy Collins, April Dawkins, Lucy Santos Green, Alli Harper, Cynthia Richardson Johnson, and Sherry Neal. 2022. "Home." Get Ready, Stay Ready. www.getreadystayready.info/home.

Calzada, Becky, Val Edwards, and Maegan Coffin Heindel. 2024. *Prepared Libraries, Empowered Teams: A Workbook for Navigating Intellectual Freedom Challenges Together*. American Library Association.

Carey, Maya Henson. 2024. "Pride Month: Public Libraries in the Crosshairs."
Southern Poverty Law Center. June 18. www.splcenter.org/
hatewatch/2024/06/18/pride-month-public-libraries-crosshairs.

Chapoco, Ralph. 2024. "State Board Adopts New Policies Tying Alabama
Library Funding to Book Restrictions." *Alabama Reflector*. May 17. https://
alabamareflector.com/2024/05/17/state-board-adopts-new-policy-tying
-alabama-library-funding-to-book-restrictions.

Cloonan, Michèle Valerie. 2018. *The Monumental Challenge of Preservation:
The Past in a Volatile World*. MIT Press.

Colomina, Carme, Héctor Sánchez Margalef, and Richard Youngs. 2021. "The
Role of Libraries in Combating Disinformation." EXPO_STU(2021)653635.
European Parliament. www.europarl.europa.eu/RegData/etudes/
STUD/2021/653635/EXPO_STU(2021)653635_EN.pdf.

Cooke, Nicole A. 2019. "Leading with Love and Hospitality: Applying a Radical
Pedagogy to LIS." *Information and Learning Sciences* 120, no. 1-2: 119–32.
10.1108/ILS-06-2018-0054.

Cooke, Nicole A. 2021. "Tell Me Sweet Little Lies: Racism as a Form of Persistent Malinformation." Project Information Literacy Provocation Series.
August 11. https://projectinfolit.org/pubs/provocation-series/essays/
tell-me-sweet-little-lies.html.

Cristol, Dean, and Belinda Gimbert. 2008. "Racial Perceptions of Young
Children: A Review of Literature Post-1999." *Early Childhood Education
Journal* 36, no. 2: 201–7. https://doi.org/10.1007/s10643-008-0251-6.

Dropp, Kyle, and Brendan Nyhan. 2017. "One-Third Don't Know Obamacare
and Affordable Care Act Are the Same." *New York Times*. February 7. www
.nytimes.com/2017/02/07/upshot/one-third-dont-know-obamacare-and
-affordable-care-act-are-the-same.html.

European Commission. n.d. "Selected Articles on Disinformation." https://
ec-europa-eu.libguides.com/disinformation/research/selected_articles.

EveryLibrary Institute. 2023. "Parent Perceptions of Librarianship 2023."
www.everylibraryinstitute.org/parent_perceptions_librarians_
survey_2023.

Goek, Sara S. 2023. "Public Library Services for Strong Communities Report:
Results from the 2022 PLA Annual Survey." Public Library Association.
www.ala.org/pla/sites/ala.org.pla/files/content/data/PLA_Services_
Survey_Report_2023.pdf.

Goldberg, Michael, and Candace Wilder. 2025. "Mississippi Libraries Ordered to Delete Academic Research in Response to State Laws." *Mississippi Today.* April 8. https://mississippitoday.org/2025/04/08/mississippi-librar ies-ordered-to-delete-academic-research-in-response-to-state-laws/.

Harris, Elizabeth A., and Alexandra Alter. 2023. "Book Bans Are Rising Sharply in Public Libraries." *New York Times.* September 21. www.nytimes .com/2023/09/21/books/book-ban-rise-libraries.html.

Holmes, Jacob. 2023. "State Library Disaffiliation from ALA Not Enough for Book Banning Group." *Alabama Political Reporter.* November 13. www .alreporter.com/2023/11/13/state-library-disaffiliation-from-ala-not -enough-for-book-banning-group/.

Howell, Joel D. 2005. "Trust and the Tuskegee Experiments." In *Clio in the Clinic: History in Medical Practice*, 213–23. Oxford University Press.

IFLA International Federation of Library Associations and Institutions. 2023. "Working Together for Information Integrity: The Role of Libraries in Europe." www.ifla.org/events/working-together-for-information -integrity-the-role-of-libraries-in-europe/.

Italie, Hillel, and Kimberlee Kruesi. 2024. "Librarians Fear New Penalties, Even Prison, as Activists Challenge Books." *AP News.* April 9. https:// apnews.com/article/book-bans-libraries-lawsuits-fines-prison -0914fa6cbb2a99b540cbbd28a38179b4.

Jaeger, Paul T., Allison Jennings-Roche, Natalie Greene Taylor, Ursula Gorham, Olivia Hodge, and Karen Kettnich. 2023. "The Urge to Censor: Raw Power, Social Control, and the Criminalization of Librarianship." *The Political Librarian* 6, no. 1: 1–20. doi.org/10.7936/pollib.8711.

Jensen, Kelly. 2024. "Here's Where Library Workers are Prohibited from Their Own Professional Organization: Book Censorship News, May 24, 2024." *Book Riot.* May 24. https://bookriot.com/states-where-librarians-cannot -join-the-ala/.

Knox, Emily J. M. 2015. *Book Banning in 21st-Century America.* Beta Phi Mu Scholars Series. Rowman & Littlefield.

Lance, Keith Curry. 1994. "The Impact of School Library Media Centers on Academic Achievement." *School Library Media Quarterly* 22, no. 3. www .ala.org/sites/default/files/aasl/content/aaslpubsandjournals/slr/ed choice/SLMQ_ImpactofSchoolLibraryMediaCentersonAcademicAchieve ment_InfoPower.pdf.

Magnusson, Tasslyn. 2024. "Book Banners Take the Fight to Public Libraries." Pen America. May 7. https://pen.org/book-banners-take-the-fight-to -public-libraries/.

McDowell, Kate. 2024. "Storytelling and/as Misinformation: Storytelling Dynamics and Narrative Structures for Three Cases of COVID-19 Viral Misinformation." In *Everyday Misinformation*. Cambridge University Press. https://hdl.handle.net/2142/117174.

McDowell, Kate, and Nicole A. Cooke. 2022. "Social Justice Storytelling: A Pedagogical Imperative." *The Library Quarterly* 92, no. 4 (October): 355–78. doi.org/10.1086/721391.

Moms for Liberty. 2024. "Who We Are." www.momsforliberty.org/about/.

Morris, Williesha. 2024. "Inside the Blistering Battle over Alabama Libraries: 'Burn the Freaking Books.'" AL.com. March 7. www.al.com/ news/2024/03/inside-the-blistering-battle-over-alabama-libraries -burn-the-freaking-books.html.

Nappo, Caroline. 2024. "Dissociative States." Heterodoxy in the Stacks. February 20. https://hxlibraries.substack.com/p/dissociative-states.

Ruffo, Giancarlo, Alfonso Semeraro, Anatasia Giachanou, and Paolo Rosso. 2023. "Studying Fake News Spreading, Polarisation Dynamics, and Manipulation by Bots: A Tale of Networks and Language." *Computer Science Review* 47, Article 100531. doi.org/10.1016/j.cosrev.2022.100531.

Silver, Laura, and Janell Fetterolf. 2024. "Who Likes Authoritarianism, and How Do They Want to Change Their Government?" Pew Research Center. February 28. https://pewrsr.ch/3USevcn.

SLIDE: The School Librarian Investigation: Divergence or Evolution? 2024. "About SLIDE." https://libslide.org.

Snyder, Timothy. 2017. *On Tyranny: Twenty Lessons from the 20th Century.* Crown.

Starbird, Kate, Renée DiResta, and Matt DeButts. 2023. "Influence and Improvisation: Participatory Disinformation during the 2020 US Election." *Social Media and Society* 9, no. 2. doi.org/10.1177/ 20563051231177943.

Suppe, Ryan. 2023. "Idaho Republicans Urge Libraries to Cut Ties with Group Led by 'Marxist Lesbian' from Boise." *Idaho Statesman.* July 18. www .idahostatesman.com/news/politics-government/state-politics/ article277404133.html.

Thompson, George F. n.d. "Verbal Judo Institute." https://verbaljudo.com.

Unite Against Book Bans. n.d. "Action Toolkit." https://uniteagainstbookbans
.org/toolkit/.

Universitat Oberta de Catalunya. 2022. "Libraries Fight Against Fake News."
October 3. www.uoc.edu/en/news/2022/148-fake-news-libraries.

Vancouver Public Library. n.d. "Disinformation and Fake News." www.vpl.ca/
guide/disinformation-and-fake-news.

Vosoughi, Soroush, Deb Roy, and Sinan Aral. 2018. "The Spread of True and
False News Online." *Science* 359, no. 6389: 1146–51. doi.org/10.1126/
science.aap9559.

Woollacott, Emma. 2024. "Yes, the Bots Are Really Taking Over the Internet."
Forbes. April 16. www.forbes.com/sites/emmawoollacott/2024/04/16/
yes-the-bots-really-are-taking-over-the-internet/.

Wardle, Claire. 2020. "Understanding Information Disorder." First Draft.
September 22. https://firstdraftnews.org/long-form-article/understand
ing-information-disorder/.

Williamson, Elizabeth. 2024. "Cast as Criminals, America's Librarians Rally to
Their Own Defense." *New York Times*. February 3. www.nytimes.
com/2024/02/03/us/book-bans-librarians.html.

World Health Organization. 2020. "Managing the COVID-19 Infodemic: Promoting Healthy Behaviors and Mitigating the Harm from Misinformation and Disinformation." September 23. www.who.int/news/item/
23-09-2020-managing-the-covid-19-infodemic-promoting-healthy
-behaviours-and-mitigating-the-harm-from-misinformation-and
-disinformation.

World Health Organization. 2021. "Claire Wardle: Tackling the Infodemic."
Bulletin of the World Health Organization, 99, no. 3: 176–77. 10.2471/
BLT.21.030321.

YALSA Young Adult Library Services Association. 2015. "Core Professional
Values for the Teen Services Profession." www.ala.org/yalsa/core
-professional-values-teen-services-profession.

Yarra Plenty Regional Library. 2021. "Where's the Source?" November 1.
www.yprl.vic.gov.au/blogs/where-s-the-source/.

Conclusion

Stories are refined through retelling. They gather wisdom over time. Interaction with audiences leads tellers to incorporate responses, so that stories that last incorporate audiences' wisdom. Think of stories that have lasted hundreds or thousands of years and the wisdom traditions that they represent. When we tell stories, we live with the humble awareness that our stories may not last and the intriguing possibility that they might. After all, most of us work in libraries created before we were born, and most will last after we are gone. We speak for libraries as those before us spoke: sustaining and stewarding them, opening their doors, and always broadening their inclusion.

Data storytelling is still new, but I have been fortunate to be part of building a library data storytelling tradition since 2017, when we first taught data storytelling at the iSchool at Illinois. Beyond the classroom, live interaction with almost a thousand library-focused audience members has contributed immeasurably to the stories told here. Audience members were present—online or in person—at talks that I gave over two years of developing these ideas. What started as a data storytelling course in an information school became a series of grants and workshops aimed at bringing the best and most current ideas about data storytelling to audiences of library workers—staff and librarians—in public, academic, school, and other libraries. One hundred people also contributed their time and expertise with interviews for the Storytelling at Work project. In every sense, the book you read here would not exist without productive, informative, and delightfully lively interactions with libraries and librarians of every kind.

Distilling wisdom from stories has been the work of generations of folklorists. However, this book represents the first attempt to distill wisdom from people working in libraries and the thousands of stories told to justify the existence and funding of libraries—in grant applications, evaluation reports, news stories, and more. The distilled wisdom in the folklore of library justification has now entered an era of extensive datafication of the public sphere in an information society. The Data Storytelling Toolkit for Libraries (DSTL) was funded by the Institute of Museum and Library Services (IMLS) to make data storytelling accessible, intuitive, and inspiring for library workers, and despite recent disruption of the IMLS, the DSTL remains available and the project will continue (McDowell, n.d.). This book and the DSTL are both ways of distilling the folklore of library justification from hundreds of stories. In other words, these are new ways of framing what we have been doing all along, conveying the wisdom of community information work as service.

The invitation here is for us all to become storytellers, honoring and amplifying the traditions of librarianship that have been the most inclusive, the most hopeful, the most radiantly successful. This is your invitation to see your data as story-worthy, to go out to your audiences, and to amplify your own messages. There is room for every variety of voices in libraries, for ways of knowing that live long lives through stories told again and again. These stories connect the books we love, the data we live, and the stories of our lives.

REFERENCE

McDowell, Kate. n.d. "The Data Storytelling Toolkit for Libraries." https://uiucdstl.wixsite.com/uiucdstl.

About the Author

Kate McDowell regularly teaches both storytelling and data storytelling courses and was the 2022 recipient of the ASIS&T Outstanding Information Science Teacher Award. She researches and publishes in the areas of storytelling as information research, social justice storytelling, and what library storytelling can teach the information sciences about data storytelling. Her projects engage contexts such as libraries, nonprofit fundraising, health misinformation, social justice in libraries, and others. McDowell has worked with regional, national, and international nonprofits, including the Pan-American Health Organization, the Public Library Association, and the Research Institute for Public Libraries. Her nationally funded project, the Data Storytelling Toolkit for Libraries, with co-PI Matthew Turk, is currently under development (imls.gov/grants/awarded/re-250094-ols-21). McDowell's storytelling research has involved training collaborations with both the University of Illinois at Urbana-Champaign and the University of Illinois system (Chicago, Springfield); storytelling consulting work for multiple nonprofits (including the 50th anniversary of the statewide Prairie Rivers Network that protects Illinois waterways); and regular storytelling workshops for the Consortium of Academic and Research Libraries in Illinois. She formerly served as the interim associate dean for academic affairs and as assistant dean for student affairs at the Illinois iSchool and has led multiple transformative projects there.

Index

V

vaccines, 116–117
Vancouver Public Library, 114
Verbal Judo, 136
Vosoughi, Soroush, 115

W

Wardle, Claire, 114–115
Weinstein, Arnold, 57
White, L. S., 28
white supremacy movements, 56

Wilder, Candace, 121
Wilkerson, Isabel, 95
Williamson, Elizabeth, 121
Woollacott, Emma, 114
World Health Organization, 116, 118
Wright, S., 28

Y

YALSA, 125
Yang, K. Wayne, xxiii
Yarra Plenty Regional Library, 114